Micro-Resilience

"What do you get when an Olympic champion and a seasoned CEO coauthor a book? Bonnie and Allen redefine how we understand competitiveness and high performance achievement. A one-two punch that will be a game changer in everything you touch."

—Tommy Spaulding, *New York Times* bestselling author of *The Heart-Led Leader* and *It's Not Just Who You Know*

"Bonnie St. John and Allen Haines have focused on how to increase hour-by-hour resilience, which is critical in today's world. Their approach integrates science-based, intentional and immediate recoveries and has broad application to health care and other service industries that count on teams to deliver their best. Micro-Resilience is a great example of a 21st century solution to meet our 21st century challenges and opportunities."

—Bernard J. Tyson, Chairman and CEO, Kaiser Permanente

"If we can't slow down the pace of modern life, then our best hope for wellness is to get better at prevention. After six years of research and testing with real people, Bonnie and Allen give us a fresh, practical program full of immediately effective, proactive tools to keep you going every day, all day long."

—Susie Ellis, Chairman & CEO, Global Wellness Institute

"*Every time I hear Bonnie speak, I come away inspired. In this book, she shares what she has learned about self-management from both a science perspective and from competing at the highest Olympic levels.* Micro-Resilience *will help you too.*"

—Dr. Henry Cloud, bestselling author of
The Power of the Other

"*Let's face it: when life is overwhelming, we want relief and we want it now!* Micro-Resilience *offers specific, easy-to-take actions that focus energy, renew energy, and retain energy over what seems out of control. Readable. Repeatable. And Reusable. You'll want to buy copies for all those you care about!*"

—Eileen McDargh, international speaker and author of seven books including *Your Resiliency GPS: A Guide for Growing through Life & Work*

"*Read + Heed the inspirational stories and insights shared in* Micro-Resilience. *Doing so will result in you having the courage to face adversity plus the confidence to manage, adapt, and respond to whatever 'disruptions' life sends your way.*"

—Kevin Carroll, author of *The Red Rubber Ball*, Creativity Katalyst for Nike, NHL, Starbucks, and many others

MICRO-RESILIENCE

MINOR SHIFTS FOR MAJOR BOOSTS IN FOCUS, DRIVE, AND ENERGY

**BONNIE ST. JOHN
ALLEN P. HAINES**

piatkus

PIATKUS

First published in Great Britain in 2017 by Piatkus

1 3 5 7 9 10 8 6 4 2

Copyright © 2017 Bonnie St John
Illustrations by Naomi Rosenblatt

The moral right of the author has been asserted.

The individual case studies in this book are based on interviews with real
people who participated in our Micro-Resilience program. We have changed their names,
geographical locations, and occupations to conceal their identities and maintain their
privacy. In some places we have compressed chronology and created composite
stories to efficiently convey the results of our research.

This book is not intended as a substitute for the medical advice
of your GP. The reader should regularly consult with their GP in
matters relating to his/her health and particularly with respect to any
symptoms that may require diagnosis or medical attention. Before
beginning any new exercise program it is highly recommended
that you seek medical advice from your GP.

The authors have made every effort to ensure the
accuracy of the information within this book was correct at
time of publication. The authors do not assume and hereby disclaim
any liability to any party for any loss, damage, or disruption caused by
errors or omissions, whether such errors or omissions result
from accident, negligence, or any other cause.

A CIP catalogue record for this book
is available from the British Library.

ISBN 978-0-349-41627-4

Printed and bound in Great Britain by Clays Ltd, St Ives plc

Papers used by Piatkus are from well-managed forests
and other responsible sources.

This book is dedicated to
Paul K. Haines (1924–2015)
and his wife of sixty-seven years,
Madlyn A. Haines.
Their lives are a testament to the kind of resilience
we can only hope to achieve.

Contents

3 RESET YOUR PRIMITIVE ALARMS: STOP YOUR EMOTIONS FROM BEING HIJACKED

Preface

Bonnie Then, and Now

For me, this book on resilience is very personal. As a five-year-old who had just come out of the hospital minus one foot and with a new artificial leg, I was mostly focused on my fancy new shoes. They were blue suede with red stitching. Until that day, the only shoes I'd ever owned were ugly white orthopedic ones with heavy steel braces.

I had no idea I would become the first African American to win medals in Winter Olympic competition. Growing up in San Diego, I had never even seen snow!

My transformation into an Olympic athlete demanded *physical resilience* far beyond what I needed to walk again. At a time when few people used gyms— especially not women and people with disabilities—I ignored the standard expectations for a one-legged, low-income black girl and trained myself to compete as a skier. Eventually I talked my way into a full scholarship to Burke Mountain Academy, a high school in Vermont for elite ski racers. At Burke I sweated side by side with the best of the best and became physically powerful for the first time in my life.

But when I reflect on my overall journey, the *mental resilience* it took to become an international skiing champion feels even more significant than all the physical work. At many junctures, I had to do things I'd never seen anyone like me do, and go places people like me never went. After numerous setbacks, like breaking both my legs in my first semester at Burke (first the real one, then, six weeks later, the artificial one), I rekindled my vision, manufactured a new batch of optimism, and refused to give up.

Beyond the physical and mental challenges, I needed a great deal of *spiritual resilience* as well. When I look at that picture of a little girl home from the hospital with the Pinocchio-style wooden leg, I see what others cannot. That little girl came back to a home where her stepfather continued to sexually abuse her for years. We struggled financially; our clothes mostly came from thrift stores or garage sales. My mother attempted suicide more than once. The emotional traumas from my childhood have tentacles that still reach deep into my relationships with people in authority, my extended family, and, of course, my husband. For decades I worked with numerous tools and techniques to help pave my own road to recovery. Only recently have I begun to repair my broken concept of "home" and enjoy the kind of core comforts others take for granted.

In my previous books, I recounted at length many of these very personal stories of disability, big dreams, and positivity. *How Strong Women Pray* looks unflinchingly at my story of emotional healing set against a backdrop of twenty-seven other women's connections to spiritual strength during life's toughest moments. *Live Your Joy* covers nine hard-won lessons I learned about confidence, high aspirations, authenticity, and relationships. *How Great Women Lead*, written with my then-teenage daughter Darcy, takes you with us on our mother-daughter journey into the lives and life lessons of amazing leaders like Hillary Clinton, Sheryl Sandberg, President Ellen Johnson Sirleaf, and many more.

After these three books, *Micro-Resilience* feels like the message I am truly destined to deliver as the culmination of my unusual life. My personal and professional worlds would be in shambles if I didn't have a substantial capacity to bounce back from extraordinary challenges. I feel that I must pass along this torch of wisdom to others.

This book builds on everything I gleaned from my experiences and expands on them. The writing here is in collaboration with my husband, Allen, who had his own journey of resilience. He navigated his way to a successful career in the cutthroat atmosphere of Hollywood studio politics despite a barrage of setbacks and disappointments along the way. Like so many of us, Allen has also suffered through the anguish of divorce and had to rebuild his life afterward.

Along with our extraordinary team at the Blue Circle Institute, Allen and I spent the last seven years distilling research, galvanizing our point of view, delivering the program to thousands of people, assessing its impact, and honing our ideas and techniques. We curated numerous research-backed micro adjustments into five Frameworks and spent hundreds of hours interviewing people to find the easiest, most effective ways to apply our tools in real-world settings. Fortune 100 executives and their teams, leaders of nonprofits, health-care professionals, entrepreneurs, educators, even stay-at-home parents have enjoyed significant benefits from using this program. In the chapters that follow, we share their stories to illustrate each aspect of our Micro-Resilience program.

Allen and I learned firsthand that these small micro-resilience changes in our lives make us stronger when we are up...or down. Not everyone should have to work as hard as we did to figure these things out, but life doesn't come with an instruction manual. You will find in these pages the greatest gift we can give from the deepest place in our souls: a practical, easy-to-use guide to living a more resilient life. If you would like to learn more about our virtual process for delivering this program, and perhaps even learn to teach Micro-Resilience yourself, please visit us at: www.microresilience.com. It is our hope that this material provides the keys you need to unlock the magic and power inherent in you from the moment you were born.

Bonnie St. John
Windham, New York
May 2016

MICRO-
RESILIENCE

1

Introduction to Micro-Resilience

Luck is not chance—
It's toil—
Fortune's expensive smile
Is earned—

—*Emily Dickinson*

ELAINE'S STORY

If you met Elaine at a dinner party, you'd think she's one of those people who somehow figured out a way to have it all. You'd hear her talk about what a supportive partner she has in her husband, Kevin. She'd have a dozen stories to tell you about her kids, four-year-old Jane and two-year-old Henry. And she'd be proud to announce that she's running the final lap in the race to make partner in her full-service corporate law firm. Confronted with such high achievement, some men might want to believe that Elaine doesn't *really* deliver the goods. They might think she was able to rise so high in her firm only because the partners wanted to show a lack of gender bias. Similarly, some women might try to convince themselves that Elaine hasn't *really* told the whole story; she must have some deep-seated unhappiness or some hidden character flaw that she's reluctant to reveal. But still, to all outward appearances, Elaine is a superwoman. She apparently embodies the cliché that all you have to do is "lean in."

Dig deeper into her story, though, and you find the truth: Elaine is a hair-on-fire workaholic.

During our busy times it's not unusual to get into work at eight o'clock in the morning and not leave until two a.m., six or seven days a week, for two or three months on end. In my line of business, it's in your face all the time: get it done, get it done, get it done! And then I still have to find time to be a good wife and mother!

I'm used to going all out until I crash and I'm dead, over and over. I put forth 110 percent and want *everything* to be A-plus quality when I do it. I'm an all-or-nothing person. If I say, "I'm in," I don't just ante up and see the other players' bets. I push all my chips across the table.

Elaine subscribed to a common fallacy among type A personalities: more work equals better work. The only way to succeed is to drive yourself until you hit a brick wall—and then do it again. Rest is for losers. A large international law firm (along with many other types of high-stakes businesses) traditionally demands this kind of work ethic. It is common practice for firms like this to engage their workforce in a kind of survival-of-the-fittest competition so they can weed out the "slackers."

Anything less than complete dedication implies a lack of strength and commitment that translates into less value to the organization. Thus people like Elaine come to believe that the only way to prosper is to put in more hours than the next person and make sure everybody knows it.

Elaine wasn't just heading for burnout: she was on course for thermonuclear conflagration. And by the time she came to us for help, the fuse was lit.

> Unlike most lawyers at big firms, I spend 100 percent of my time focused on one large government organization. This client represents more than forty-five thousand billable hours per annum and is the firm's largest single client. The contract is coming up for renewal, and we have to compete with other firms who are dying to take the business away from us. Our team—including forty partners and more than three hundred associates, clerks, paralegals, and others—only has forty-five days to create a detailed, five-hundred-page response to the RFP [request for proposal], which is worth more than $100 million.
>
> Did I say there is a lot riding on this? Basically, if we win this proposal I have a clear path

to promotion into partnership. And if we don't win this proposal...I have to find a new client. I don't want to be dramatic about it, but my whole career is pretty much riding on the next forty-five days.

A UNIVERSAL CONDITION

Elaine is a perfectionist as well as competitive by nature, so it was almost impossible for her to see a course of action other than the one she was used to—*drive until you drop*. And she's not alone. It doesn't matter if you work in a high-pressure corporate environment, sell real estate, tend bar, heal the sick, or toil as a full-time parent, the pace of our information-driven, globally connected twenty-first-century society forces us to accelerate down the tracks of modern life—and most of us feel dangerously close to flying off the rails. Rampant corporate "rightsizing" often demands twice as much from half the number of people. Our children boomerang back home after college while at the same time our parents need our support as they hit their golden years. We multitask ourselves into oblivion just to keep up. We push, we strive, we conquer!

And then we collapse.

Can we keep this up? Not if we continue to live exactly as we have up to this point. Like Elaine, we often drive ourselves past the point of exhaustion and then hope to catch up in the evenings, on weekends, or with a vacation. But often the bits of rest we do manage to achieve are co-opted by an array of technology that blips and bleeps with e-mail, text messages, Facebook updates, Instagrams, Snapchats, and whatever else keeps us plugged in 24-7.

So what do we do? Since the outward forces that exert stress on us are unlikely to disappear, our only choice is to look *inward* at ways we can better harness our natural human resources and adapt to the environment. We need to find a work-around that allows us to achieve the resilience we need to more quickly and efficiently bounce back when we inevitably get knocked off course. If the speed of life won't slow down, we need to speed up our recoveries to stay ahead.

DEFINING RESILIENCE

In a *Harvard Business Review* article entitled "Surprises Are the New Normal; Resilience Is the New Skill," world-renowned sociologist and Harvard Business School professor Rosabeth Moss Kanter defines resilience as "the new skill" for the contemporary workforce. The ability to be resilient is not just "nice to have," it has now become a "must have."[1]

That's what this book is all about: resilience.

But our definition of "resilience" is different from the word's traditional meaning. According to *Dictionary.com*, resilience is "the power or ability to return to the original form...after being bent, compressed, or stretched." Think of a sponge. When you squeeze a sponge, it will always spring back to its normal shape. But we believe that normal is not good enough; we focus instead on ways to bounce back *better than normal*.

Our approach differs from traditional notions of resilience in another important respect. When we tell people that our work is about helping our clients stay resilient, they often say, "I know someone who is very resilient; she bounced back from _____." You can fill in the blank: cancer, hurricane, divorce, or any other major ordeal that qualifies as something difficult to recover from. These extreme scenarios can be devastating, and a lot of support is available to help you manage these catastrophic events. But instead of taking the macro view of resilience—the long view, encompassing a process that often takes many years—we chose to exclusively study the day-by-day, hour-by-hour challenges of resilience. Our focus is on the ordinary interactions with friends, family, and coworkers that throw us into conscious or unconscious turmoil. For most of us, the hundreds of miniature bruises we experience each day determine the overall quality of our lives far more dramatically than the giant traumas that punctuate the decades.

Research conducted by Dr. James Loehr—a respected sports psychologist, author of *The Power of Full Engagement*, and the founder of the Johnson & Johnson Human Performance Institute in Orlando, Florida—intrigued us.[2] Jim decided to find out what he could learn by studying athletes who dominated the world-class tennis circuit. He wanted to understand why there were hundreds of players on international tours but only a handful of champions who consistently took home the trophies. What made the difference for the athletes in this top tier? What are the habits that enable breakthrough performance under intense competitive pressure? Jim performed all sorts of analyses, but to his frustration, he couldn't find any consistent differences among the best players.

Until he looked at what they did *between the points*.

A pattern jumped out immediately. As he sifted

through several hours of video, Jim noticed that the top athletes exhibited very similar habits when they returned to the baseline after scoring and when they retired courtside between games and sets. These distinct, identifiable between-the-points behaviors were common to the winners and centered on energy recovery and positive focus. Jim put heart-rate monitors on these top players and found that they were able to bring their heart rates back to an ideal zone more quickly and efficiently than less successful competitors. The further he went down the list of seeded players, the more dramatic the differences were. Those at the bottom of the list employed almost none of these rejuvenating behaviors. They stayed keyed up, tense, and even distracted in the sixteen to twenty seconds that normally elapse between a point scored and the following serve.[3]

Jim used his discoveries to revolutionize sports training. He developed a series of focus exercises and relaxation techniques that teach players to shake off mistakes, release tension, project a confident image to their opponents, and establish rituals to increase consistency. Jim's program, called the 16-Second Cure, is now an essential element of tennis coaching throughout the world.

Jim and his tennis players really got us thinking. He learned that by the last set of a three-hour tennis match, the competitor who had been using small, sometimes barely noticeable mini recoveries—what we began to call *Micro-Resilience*—between the points was likely to play much closer to the best of his or her ability than the player who didn't. We began to think that micro-resilience was more than a way to help professional athletes recover energy on the tennis court: it also could help the rest of us develop the kinds of comeback skills we need to combat the blitzkrieg of stress in our lives. What if we all could stay closer to playing our A game all day, every day, by recharging our batteries as we go?

THE FIVE FRAMEWORKS

It turns out we really *can* retrain our brains, recharge our bodies, and adapt our lifestyles to meet twenty-first-century demands. We scoured research in the fields of neuroscience, psychology, and physiology to understand the specific forces that sap our energy. We then created a set of five strategies that can get us back on track quickly and efficiently.

In our workshops, we call these techniques "Frameworks" because they involve a new way of looking at our lives—a way of perceiving situations and framing problems that break us out of our old patterns of thinking.

All these techniques are designed to speed up our daily recoveries "between points":

1. **Refocus** Your Brain

2. **Reset** Your Primitive Alarms

3. **Reframe** Your Attitude

4. **Refresh** Your Body

5. **Renew** Your Spirit

Together they comprise micro-resilience—a set of minor shifts you can make throughout your day that yield major boosts in your energy and productivity.

MICRO SUPPORTS MACRO

It's crucial to recognize that micro-resilience is different from what we refer to as macro-resilience—the set of more time-consuming habits, such as exercise, meditation, and careful nutrition, that give us increased energy and better health over the long term. Micro-resilience is in no way a substitute for these critical building blocks of physical and mental health. But macro processes take weeks and often months of diligent, consistent work to show results, and implementing this sustained attention is often where we fail. We fantasize that "someday" we will find time to make our macro investment in health, but our goalposts keep moving forward. How many times have you heard (or said), "I'll do it when we move into a new house...when I get promoted...when the kids go to college"?

Micro-resilience, on the other hand, takes almost no time and works immediately—hour by hour, day by day. You can use micro-resilience right now, as you read, and see results. In a world where we stand impatiently tapping a foot in front of a microwave, it's important to provide an approach that fits into our instant-everything culture.

Micro- and macro-resilience mutually reinforce each other, too. No matter how perfectly you maintain good health behaviors, you will still be hit with all sorts of challenges on a daily basis. That unusually horrific day at work can make even the most diligent of us plop down in front of the TV to recover with a bag of chips or a quart of ice cream instead of with more nourishing options. Micro-resilience techniques can make that day feel less exhausting and, at the end, leave you more inclined to stay on a positive macro trajectory—to make healthful food choices, exercise, sleep better, and more easily interact with friends and family. Micro-resilience behaviors, when repeated daily, foster a cumulative macro effect.

MICRO-RESILIENCE IN ACTION

We explained to Elaine that using micro-resilience isn't about weakness. On the contrary, these small adjustments would help her "better her best" and perform closer to her world-class capability. Repeatedly working to the point of collapse over the course of those crucial forty-five days wasn't going to be good enough to get the job done at the level she needed. Her bleary eyes and foggy brain would eventually bring her to the point of diminishing returns. She would begin to introduce errors and inconsistencies that would require even more effort to repair. Conversely, though, strategic recoveries along the way could allow her to achieve a new and higher level of the all-in commitment she values so highly. Some alternative "between-the-points" options soon began to take shape.

By three p.m. on Monday, I'd been sitting at my computer for seven hours and still had many

more hours of work to do to prepare the project plan for the partners' kickoff call early the next morning. Because I had learned about micro-resilience, though, I saw that I had a choice. I could continue to grind through it, or I could put my kids in the jogging stroller, take a break from it all, and come back with a fresh mind. That's something I would never, ever have considered before.

Well...it was great! I spent time laughing with my kids, doing something physical, getting fresh air, and clearing my head. Back at my desk I used the Refocus Your Brain tools to organize my ideas. Later I took another break to read a story to my kids and tuck them into bed.

In the end, the work came out much better than if I had just sat at my desk slogging away at it. Taking micro breaks seems counterintuitive, but I've learned that it really works.

All-in performance now looks different on the teams Elaine leads. She still works very hard and drives her people to do the same, but she encourages everyone around her to use a variety of micro-resilience strategies to bolster their health, positivity, and brainpower. With this approach, she and her group are sharper, clearer, and more efficient than they were when they pushed themselves beyond their breaking points. Even under the most demanding circumstances, using micro-resilience modifications "between the points," as you proceed from challenge to challenge throughout your day, can make the difference between an engaging, invigorating work-place you look forward to being part of and a Dickensian nightmare you can't wait to leave.

One of our participants put it this way:

> **This work is more than its individual parts: it's the way all the Frameworks come together. Keeping micro-resilience in front of you every day—making it part of your daily habits, your routine, part of the fabric of your life—is huge. It's what sets it apart. To break resilience up into little pieces and have these pieces become part of who you are makes all the difference.**

These adjustments do not take hours of your time or draw your focus away from important things that need your attention. Our bite-size but extremely powerful tweaks work *with* you to incrementally adjust your habits and restore your energy.

Micro-resilience honors our lives as they are. We do not need to change, but we do need to evolve. These simple, research-backed concepts allow us to accept whatever setbacks we experience and bounce back with strength, energy, and positivity—better than before. Employing a fresh strategy to recover between stressful episodes in our lives turns out to be easy.

It also happens to be supremely satisfying.

1. Rosabeth Moss Kanter, "Surprises Are the New Normal; Resilience Is the New Skill," *Harvard Business Review* (July 2013).
2. Jim Loehr and Tony Schwartz, *The Power of Full Engagement* (New York: Simon and Schuster, 2003).
3. James Loehr, in discussion with the author, 2014.

2

Refocus Your Brain

Think, Organize, and Execute More Effectively

You have brains in your head. You have feet in your shoes.
You can steer yourself any direction you choose.

—Dr. Seuss

GREG'S STORY

Greg is a miracle worker. He labors tirelessly to integrate an array of sophisticated mechanical and electronic elements into devices that allow, as they say, "the lame to walk." Greg builds prosthetic limbs—specifically artificial legs—and he does his job with almost fanatical precision. Each prosthetic device is unique to the user and therefore requires a host of customizations and fine-tuning. When Greg provides you with a new leg, you can be sure he's done everything he can to make it fit as comfortably and as naturally as possible. When you see a person with a prosthetic limb of any kind run a marathon, dance at a wedding, or just smoothly walk down the street, please appreciate the unsung hard work and dedication of miracle workers like Greg.

Greg's profession is intense. It requires a high degree of focus and concentration: not only does he care for patients and construct sensitive devices that unite human mechanics and technology, he also runs a business that requires him to negotiate with the huge bureaucracies in government and insurance companies. Each of these endeavors requires a unique skill set, and sometimes he doesn't know where he should put his attention first.

> A lot of things pile up, you know? I'm scheduled to be on a conference call with corporate headquarters in fifteen minutes, there's a patient in the examination room who is very needy, the office staff is asking me about billing codes, and at the same time urgent phone calls are coming in from other patients...I just can't always keep all those balls up in the air.
>
> I get this kind of emotional intensity where I feel trapped. You can't back away. Ultimately, things have to get done. Right? But it's unpleasant, and sometimes you say things that you don't necessarily want to say, or that you wish you hadn't said. And then other people in the office get kind of huffy, too, because I got huffy. It's what I call an "energy fart" because your bad energy from that moment spills out into the office and stinks up the air.

REFOCUS YOUR BRAIN: THE SCIENCE

To understand why Greg often feels so mentally overwhelmed, let's look at how the human brain is configured. First, it is important to distinguish between the older parts of our brain and the more recently evolved sections that handle the demands of higher-order thinking. The brain stem, cerebellum, and basal ganglia—a region often called the *lizard brain* because it's quite similar to the brain of an iguana—contain the genetically oldest structures of our neural system, so these are the parts of the brain that evolved first. This lizard brain controls automatic functions in our bodies such as breathing, heartbeat, and other life-support systems, but doesn't provide mechanisms that allow us to learn, plan, or make decisions. Those functions are controlled by the most advanced portion of the brain, called the cortex.

Developmental molecular biologist Dr. John Medina, author of *Brain Rules*, describes the cortex as a type of cathedral that arches above the rest of the brain. The cortex is essentially the surface of your brain, which communicates constantly with the interior through deeply embedded electrical impulses. The word *cortex* is Latin for "bark," and just as bark is the "skin" of a tree, the cortex is the "skin" of the brain. In various parts of the brain, it can be as thin as blotting paper or as thick as heavy-duty cardboard, and it seems to be stuffed into a space that is far too small. The wrinkled nature of the cortex is actually a brilliant trick that allows more of its surface area to fit inside the confines of the cranium. If it were unfolded, it would be about the size of your favorite baby blanket.[1]

The Prefrontal Cortex and Executive Brain Function

The activities we focus on in this chapter are rooted primarily in one particular part of the cortex: the prefrontal cortex (PFC). The PFC is the most advanced segment of the most advanced section of the brain. It contains the brain's most recent and most expansive evolutionary structures, and is responsible for the cognitive functions we think of as uniquely human, such as the ability to set complex goals, plan our futures, restrain our instinctive impulses, make informed decisions, and organize our activities.[2] Collectively, these sophisticated abilities are often referred to as the *executive functions* of the brain.

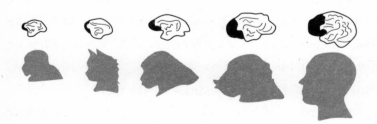

The human brain has a relatively larger PFC
than other species

Neuroscientists commonly point out that the human PFC takes up about a third of the cortical region, a proportionally much larger area than the PFC occupies in any other species. In the previous pictures, we see that the size of the PFC relative to the rest of the brain is by far the largest in humans. Although research into the mechanisms of the brain continues, it is generally accepted that humans have a significantly greater PFC capacity, and thus more executive brain function, than other animals.

Change and Evolution

Given that the PFC in humans is far more capable than that of any other species on the planet, why do we still feel mentally overtaxed so much of the time?

Consider the dramatic economic shifts that have occurred within the last hundred or so years. According to the Bureau of Labor Statistics, in the early 1900s more than 60 percent of the workforce in the United States still made tangible things with physical labor, either on farms, in factories, or through mining and construction.[3] But today that figure is less than 15 percent.[4]

By contrast, the group that management consultant and author Peter Drucker dubbed "knowledge workers" (engineers, physicians, lawyers, designers, analysts, office staff, and so on) has ballooned to gigantic proportions. Another large and growing contingent—service workers— includes people who work in food service, customer service, health care, and similar fields. In addition, more of us than ever before are living out our dreams as musicians, politicians, small-business owners, and entrepreneurs. Comparatively few of us are tied down in the production of the food we eat or the objects we need to live. One impact of this transformation is that the vast majority of our modern workforce needs more emotional intelligence (people skills) as well as more facility with abstraction (conceptual skills) than it ever needed before. Both these abilities are anchored in the PFC.

Add to these trends the rise of computers and big data. The US Census Bureau reports that 84 percent of households owned a computer of some kind in 2013. Access to the Internet connects us to large pools of information but also adds pressure to comb through this voluminous data for both work and entertainment. Even if you work at a factory job, you are likely to be using a computer for robotics, design schematics, quality control, or some other high-tech aspect of the manufacturing process. What was previously a largely physical and repetitive job now likely requires higher-order skills and, perhaps, more abstract thought.

To be clear, we are not arguing that we work harder today than our great-great-grandparents did. But during the last few centuries, the demand for executive brain function seems to have increased and become more widespread. Nevertheless, a century is only the blink of an eye on the evolutionary time scale. Since it takes anywhere from a hundred thousand to a million years for relatively minor changes to occur in existing biological structures, we could be waiting a long time for our prefrontal cortex to enlarge its capacity in response to the demands we place on it.

Multitasking is NOT the Answer

Greg's story, at the beginning of this chapter, is typical of the challenges many business leaders face. In various kinds of companies across all types of industries, we meet people who are worn out, cannot focus as well as they should, and tend to be much more reactive than strategic. They firmly believe that multitasking is the only way they can stay ahead of the myriad demands put before them. The problem is that our brains can provide us with only a finite amount of focus at any given time. Scientists such as Daniel Kahneman, author of the influential book *Attention and Effort,* have conducted research that bears this out.[5] Some scientists measure the extra burdens on the brain caused by frequent attention shifts; others document the physical strains that result from bottlenecks in the brain where simultaneous tasks compete for finite resources.[6] Multitasking is least problematic when the tasks we perform are simple and unrelated, such as walking while talking or folding laundry while watching TV.

Proficiency disintegrates rapidly, however, when we try to multitask our way through our normal workday. According to some estimates, it can easily take up to 40 percent longer to complete projects when you're interrupted than it does when you can maintain specific focus.[7] After all, it takes energy to switch gears—you have to attend to an interruption, then reacquire your focus on the original undertaking, remember where you left off, and expend additional neural resources to get yourself back on track. The more you bifurcate (or trifurcate, etc.) your attention, the more you become drained.

Performing multiple activities that involve complexities like decision making and analysis slows us down even more dramatically. When our thought process is divided, our ability to recall details diminishes. We significantly reduce impulses for creativity, and we increase the risk of serious mistakes—all of which contribute to an overall reduction in the quality of our work. A 2006 study found that even when we talk on a hands-free cell phone while driving, as millions of people believe they do quite well, the impairments are similar to those of driving drunk: slower reaction times, erratic movements, more frequent traffic accidents.[8]

John Arden, an expert in neuropsychology who oversees the training of more than one hundred interns in twenty-two medical centers for the health-care giant Kaiser Permanente, recounted the story of a patient who came to him with the complaint that her memory had been failing over the previous few years. She was afraid that she might have contracted attention deficit disorder (ADD).

After explaining that ADD was not contagious, Dr. Arden offered a solution that he hoped would minimize the chaos in her life:

I told her that it was no wonder she wasn't remembering anything, since she rarely focused attention on anything long enough to code it into her memory. We began to structure [her] day so that she was present with whatever she was doing at any given time. She learned to focus attention on each task until it was completed. Her working memory began to function

well so that she could better code information into her long-term memory.[9]

It is fine to perform two or more tasks at once if quality or accuracy is not a high priority. But the widespread belief that multitasking makes us *more* efficient in our busy lives is far more myth than science. At every business level, from the C suites to the front lines, we see rampant exhaustion and intellectual depreciation as a result of this misunderstood social norm.

REFOCUS YOUR BRAIN: SOLUTIONS

The dilemma faced by Dr. Arden's patient may seem extreme, but it's surprisingly similar to the mental quagmires faced by many of the participants in our Micro-Resilience programs. So we put together a short list of practical, research-supported, and thoroughly tested methods that help us use our precious executive brain functions more judiciously and effectively.

Zone Refocus: Create an Island in the Stream

When faced with the unceasing flow of communication that vies for our limited attention, think of a way to put yourself in a separate zone—a kind of "island in the stream." Zones can be physical—perhaps a specific area in your home or workplace where you go when you don't want to be disturbed. Zones can also be a period of time—a regular or ad hoc interlude during the day that you designate as a "quiet" or "focus" zone. Whether zones are physical or temporal, the important thing is that you create them and use them to block out distractions and interruptions during periods of concentrated focus.

You may believe that it's impossible to take even short time-outs from your particular brand of madness. We've heard some of our clients say, "My boss requires that I always answer quickly" and "Everything needs my attention immediately because my coworkers count on me." But there are work-arounds to address almost any challenge. You can arrange mutually acceptable expectations for e-mail, text messages, and phone calls that let you do your best work yet still be responsive to truly critical communications as well as to the overall flow of information throughout your organization. Your boss will probably be flexible once he or she understands the diminishing returns that result from numerous disruptions.

Communication to others about the appropriate thresholds for interruption in our zones is critical to their success. There are many creative ways to establish your boundaries. In one hospital we studied, nurses wear brightly colored sashes while they dispense medicine to ensure that there will be no intrusions, which could cause potentially fatal mistakes. One office we toured had a noisy bullpen; workers there designated a specific conference room as a silent workspace, like a quiet car on a train. Find ways to meet your needs for concentration. Some people can set up several zones per day, while others can build in only one or two per week. But whether you construct one zone or ten, you'll still experience a significant increase in productivity by using these oases of focus.

When you set and agree to flexible limits for your zones, you not only commit to them yourself, but also encourage others around you to respect and support your parameters. We've experienced this firsthand. As coauthors, we often write at the same time in close proximity. If one of us turns around and bothers the other, the disturbed writer can instantly lose a train of thought, which requires a difficult reboot back into the flow of words. So we've agreed to always ask for permission before an interruption. We both understand that the answer to "May I interrupt you?" may be a curt "No." The abrupt inflection is not meant to be offensive but rather efficient—it minimizes the distraction. Once we feel ready to pause, we politely provide an "all clear" and address our partner—unless, of course, that person has gone back to work and has put up their own virtual Do Not Enter sign.

It took us a bit of trial and error to perfect this process. Allen in particular becomes easily distracted and quickly frustrated when interrupted. In one memorable episode several years ago, Bonnie was in a wheelchair after she broke her *only* ankle in an unfortunate moped incident on the island of Nantucket. We often write in coffee shops (a zone away from the office), and we minimize the tendency to disturb each other by sitting at opposite ends of the café. Bonnie had a question for Allen, so she wheeled herself across the room and came up behind him to get his attention. He became so annoyed with her looking over his shoulder that he rather loudly ordered her to "roll away" until he finished his thought—which prompted more than a few raised eyebrows from the other java-sipping patrons. Now that we are better at communicating our limits, the zone structure provides a vast improvement in efficiency, a way to avoid potential public embarrassment, and a welcome aid to marital bliss.

Another example comes from one of the participants in our Micro-Resilience program. For more than a year, Jiang received feedback that her chances for promotion were undermined by her tendency to do too many things for too many people. She was perceived as more "worker bee" than senior leadership material. Excessive multitasking had so undermined the executive functions of her brain that she could not prove she could handle the responsibilities of an executive in her company. Establishing zones provided immediate relief.

My natural tendency is to multitask. Zones give me the space to prioritize and get myself out of panic mode. I was so out of control and frantic that I didn't enjoy my work. I apologized to the people who work for me far too often because they reminded *me* what needed to get done. Using zones has restored my sanity…and my confidence in myself. Others now see me as more in control.

It's no accident that enhanced executive brain function gives you more "executive presence" and, therefore, a better case for promotion.

Zone Refocus: Change the Culture

Constant interruptions in the office exponentially compounded Greg's multitasking challenges. To establish effective zones of concentration, the first thing he needed to do was engage his coworkers in developing a communication strategy, one that respected everyone's boundaries.

> **We're in very close quarters; we're kind of on top of each other. So it can be tempting when I have something I want to push forward and I just need one little piece of information from the others; all I have to do is turn my head and ask, regardless of whether I'm interrupting. On the other hand, I don't want them to interrupt me, and that's not fair. I have to get better at giving my coworkers zones, and if I did, I think they would respect my zones more. It's about productivity, but it's about quality of life, too.**

It is not unusual to walk a fine line between collaboration and continuous interference. In high-tech, future-forward companies, we often hear about the eradication of private offices. In some instances, we've even seen the replacement of desks assigned to a specific person in favor of impersonal cubbyholes claimed only one day at a time. An open and flexible office setup has many advantages, but the resulting breaches of privacy can dissipate mental resources. Still, we don't have to accept continuous interruptions as a fait accompli. Many people we've coached are surprised to see how negotiable boundaries can be.

We encouraged Greg to have a meeting with his staff to specifically address zones and boundaries—for him and for them. Greg told his team:

> I can tell it's really aggravating when I interrupt you, and it's hard for me to maintain my train of thought when I'm interrupted, too. Let's try to compile our questions a bit instead of shouting each one out the moment we think of it.
>
> I also need a zone for myself when I'm between patients. I often only have a few minutes after I finish with one patient before the next person comes in, so I take that time to regroup. But that doesn't mean that you can't intrude into that zone if it's critical. It's not impermeable.

Greg was careful to communicate that this new zone culture included boundaries for everyone in his organization, not just for him as the boss. He told us:

To get respect, you have to give respect. If I'm asking for it, I have to also provide it. We've been using hand signals to check whether the person we want to speak with is ready to take a question or not. It's definitely helped.

Very quickly, Greg and his team began to enjoy the benefits of their zones. Interpersonal communication became more efficient. The energy of the office became less tense. Respect for one another's boundaries quickly translated into more engaged employees and better patient care. Doing high-quality work became less exhausting.

Zone Refocus: Tips

1. Put zones on your calendar: block out a portion of time during which you will work "in the zone." Use this time to perform tasks that require accuracy, quality, and creativity.

2. Establish a quiet physical space where you can go to concentrate and be "in the zone." This may or may not require a door that you can close.

3. Communicate your boundaries to coworkers, friends, and family so they know how to interrupt you—and

under what conditions. Explain why and how you are using zones to get more done. Be sensitive to their needs as well—don't overdo your zones.

4. Use an app or a plug-in to cancel or silence alerts for e-mails, text messages, and phone calls. Most of these tools will still allow you to be reached in case of an emergency.

5. Calm and clear your mind as you transition into your zone. See page 30 for specific techniques.

Off-Load Refocus: Don't Hold It All in Your Head

Before we went to lunch with David Rock, author of *Your Brain at Work*,[10] we were already well versed in the benefits of "downloading" information from the working memory of our overextended PFCs. We'd read research on the benefits of note taking[11] and investigated the way technologies can supplement our mental resources.[12] We'd learned from our experience facilitating groups that whiteboards, flip charts, slides, and other visual aids reduce participants' need to hold many abstract concepts in their heads all at once and leave more bandwidth for analysis and creative collaboration. But David took our thinking to a whole new level with a simple demonstration of how to apply all that research to everyday life.

On a sunny spring afternoon, we met David for lunch at a charming café in midtown Manhattan. As soon as we sat down and food was ordered, he dived right into our discussion about the brain, leadership, and resilience. At the same time, he did something extraordinary that stuck with us forever. He pulled out a well-worn spiral notebook, placed it on the table between us, and began to draw thought bubbles and mind maps to illustrate the various elements of our conversation.

Neuroleadership

Self   *Team*   *Coaching*

He wasn't taking notes—these scribbles were never meant to be used for future reference. In fact, he threw them away when we were finished. David drew the visuals simply to reduce his brain clutter in the moment, nothing more.

Abstract discussions are not difficult or particularly taxing for David—or for us, either. We could have covered the same ground without the impromptu graphics. This extra scaffolding, however, supported our memories and conserved our mental energy for lively debate and cognitive connections. It made us more likely to have a rich, productive conversation. It also meant less brain fatigue as we moved down the long list of intellectual tasks we had to undertake during the rest of our day.

We all tend to take for granted the ability to envision, invent, plan, and reorganize on the fly, but this kind of activity taxes us more than we realize. A continuous, albeit small, reduction in mental effort can provide a palpable boost in the quality of our thoughts over the long haul. David showed us what "off-loading" can look like, even in something as seemingly undemanding as a lunchtime conversation.

David's use of off-loading reminded us of a story we'd heard about Albert Einstein. A colleague once asked the professor for his phone number, and he reached for the telephone directory to look it up.

"You are reputed to be the most intelligent man in the world, but you can't remember your own phone number?" the man asked him, flabbergasted.

"No," answered Einstein. "Why should I memorize something I can so easily get from a book?"

Off-Load Refocus: Tips

1. Make a habit of off-loading frequently—draw idea bubbles on paper during meetings, take notes, or

use a whiteboard to think through decisions. During conversations, place these creations where everyone can see them.

2. "To-do" lists are an obvious means of off-loading that most of us already use for efficiency.

3. Keep a small notebook (paper or smartphone) with you everywhere you go and use it to jot down sudden inspirations and map your thinking.

4. Keep a record of your idea bubbles and whiteboard notes by taking pictures of them on your smartphone. This way, those nuggets of information will be always at hand.

5. Remember that even if you don't save your notes, the process of taking them raises the quality of your thinking.

Decision Refocus: Watch the Timing, Reduce the Quantity

A judge, a social worker, and a criminologist were interviewing three prisoners in an Israeli jail.

This sounds like the beginning of a bad joke, but it's actually a true story about a research project reported by the *New York Times* in the following way.[13] All three of the Israeli prisoners had completed two-thirds of their sentences, but only one of them was granted parole. Which one do you think it was?

1. An Arab Israeli serving a thirty-month sentence for fraud (case heard at 8:50 a.m.)

2. A Jewish Israeli serving a sixteen-month sentence for assault (case heard at 3:10 p.m.)

3. An Arab Israeli serving a thirty-month sentence for fraud (case heard at 4:25 p.m.)

It seems likely that the judge, who was Jewish, would have released the Jewish prisoner. Even if we don't assume an ethnic bias, the second prisoner had the least time left to serve.

In the true story of the three prisoners, however, only the first prisoner was granted freedom. But if the first prisoner was let go, why not the third one, who'd committed the identical crime and served the identical sentence?

"There was a pattern to the parole board's decisions," observed John Tierney, author of the *Times* article, "but it wasn't related to the men's ethnic backgrounds, crimes or sentences. It was all about timing." Researchers Jonathan Levav of Stanford and Shai Danziger of Ben-Gurion University analyzed 1,112 cases that came before eight judges and found that the chances of receiving parole started at about 65 percent in the morning, then fell to nearly zero before the judges went out for a snack break or lunch. After the break, the probability of parole shot back up to 65 percent once again, then showed a steady decline until the next break or the end of the day.

Prisoner 1, lucky enough to have his case heard at 8:50 in the morning, enjoyed much higher odds for a positive result. Prisoners 2 and 3 probably stayed in prison longer simply because they'd had the misfortune to come before the judge in the late afternoon. With tremendous understatement, Levav and Danziger concluded, "Our findings suggest that judicial rulings can be swayed by extraneous variables that should have no bearing on legal decisions."

These findings are supported by numerous studies showing that the ability to make a large number of decisions in close succession is easily compromised as time goes on—a phenomenon often referred to as "decision fatigue."[14] According to experts, however, our mental acuity, often more fragile than we think it is, can be restored by some very easy countermeasures, such as viewing scenes of nature,[15] stopping for short periods of rest,[16] inducing positive mood shifts,[17] and increasing glucose levels in the body.[18]

Another study, conducted in 2014, demonstrated that doctors tend to overprescribe antibiotics as the day wears on, even when medical observation suggests that the drugs may not be necessary.[19] Nurses we interviewed told us that most people who are addicted to painkillers know to visit doctors only at the end of the day so they are more likely to get their fix with little scrutiny. If the decisions of judges and doctors—highly educated, experienced, wise men and women whom we trust to make life-and-death assessments—can be so clearly influenced by the time of day or the time since they've eaten, our mental output must certainly be vulnerable to such vicissitudes as well.

Decision Refocus: Tips

1. Make your important decisions early in the day or after you invigorate yourself with food, rest, or something to help you feel more positive (see page 103 for suggestions).

2. Pay attention to not only your decision-fatigue level, but also that of others on your team. If the need to

make an important decision arises just before lunch or at the end of the day, make an effort to postpone it or revisit it when everyone is fresh.

3. Simplify your office, your wardrobe, your house, and your routines whenever possible so that everyday tasks require fewer decisions. For example, as the number of days Bonnie spent on the road grew, she simplified her packing. Now she wears only black skirts, black tops, and black shoes, an ensemble that she brightens with jewelry and jackets in red, teal, salmon, and other vivid colors. This saves enormous time as she packs, gets dressed, and manages dry cleaning.

4. Train others on your team to take on more decision-making responsibility. Micromanaging coworkers trains them *not* to make decisions and encourages them to bother you about every little thing. Distributed decision authority—with adequate support and preparation—is most compatible with sustained high performance.

5. Use checklists for decisions that you make repeatedly. Checklists can save time, preserve mental energy, and increase accuracy. Use them to decide which employee to hire, what belongs in the quarterly report, or which items belong on your next grocery

list. Did you ever get to the gym and discover that you'd forgotten your sneakers? A gym-day checklist eliminates the process of deciding what to bring.

Don't confuse checklists with simple to-do lists, which are memory aids that you throw away after you've completed all the items. A checklist can be used again and again, is revised over time, and helps reduce the amount of evaluation and analysis required for a particular task. In his book *The Checklist Manifesto*, prominent surgeon Dr. Atul Gawande draws attention to breakthrough-quality improvements put in place by hospitals that use checklists for everything from infection prevention to surgical procedures:

Checklists seem able to defend anyone, even the experienced, against failure in many more tasks than we realized. They provide a kind of cognitive net. They catch mental flaws inherent in all of us—flaws of memory and attention and thoroughness.[20]

Gawande admits he didn't *really* believe that the quality of his own surgical work would improve with checklists; he developed the policies for *other* surgeons. With great candor, however, he reveals several examples of errors—serious problems—that were avoided in his own practice once he instituted checklists. Even among smart and highly trained medical professionals, the crutch of a checklist preserves scarce decision-making resources for their most important uses.

6. "Prioritize prioritizing," advises David Rock, because this is one of the brain's most energy-guzzling processes. Even a few minutes of an attention-rich task, such as answering e-mail, may leave you with too few resources left to prioritize properly.[21] Prioritization involves a long series of decisions about abstract ideas that you must hold all at once in your working memory. So prioritize only when fresh and uninterrupted, and use visual aids: color-code various categories, or use flash cards, Post-its, or other organizational tools to help move elements into the right order. Since prioritization is so difficult to do well, bring all of the brain-boost ideas we have presented to bear on it.

Exercise Refocus: Use Movement to Improve Thinking

When a midlife crisis hits, we may feel a deep sense of remorse for goals not accomplished, face an increasing awareness of mortality, yearn for our lost youth, or try to right what we perceive as wrongs we committed earlier in life. But when world-renowned neuroscientist Wendy Suzuki had a midlife crisis, she began a new line of research and wrote a best-selling book about her personal transformation: *Healthy Brain, Happy Life.*[22] She also threw herself into a new exercise routine. As she did so, she made a startling discovery: it was easier to write grant proposals and scientific papers after she began to work out at the gym regularly.

> **Whereas it usually took me a week to write just one section of a grant application, I was now drafting more efficiently, fine-tuning more quickly, and enjoying the process a whole lot more. My attention was more focused and my thinking was clearer. I made deeper, more substantive connections between my ideas and was doing so far sooner in the process than usual.**

The concept that exercise is good for your body isn't news. The connection between exercise and the brain, however, is a much less explored area of research—and it completely seized Wendy's imagination. She now devotes all her efforts to studying the effects of exercise on memory, creativity, mood, and other brain functions. Much of what she is doing relates to what we call macro-resilience—in this case the benefits of consistent workouts over months and months.

But there are several studies to support the notion that exercise *today* can make your brain work better *today*. In a combination of four experiments conducted at Stanford University in 2014, researchers Marily Oppezzo and Daniel Schwartz showed that creativity dramatically increased during walking—and that the effects persisted after the walking stopped.[23] As part of the experiment, they tested outdoor walks in bright sunshine against indoor walks in bleak surroundings and found no difference in the results; only the walking matters, not the environment.

Another study tested students at a large urban college after a twenty-minute dance class and found significant improvements in their flexibility of thinking, expression of ideas, and generation of original thoughts.[24] A breakthrough high school program in Illinois took students who were behind their grade level in reading and gave them a special exercise class every morning. Those students improved their scores at nearly double the rate of the students who took a standard phys-ed class in the afternoon.[25] Overall, exercise generates significant same-day improvement in high-order thinking skills that remain measurable after the exercise ends. Benefits include faster mental processes, enhanced memory storage and retrieval, better selective attention,[26] and more creative thinking.[27]

There are, however, important limitations to take into account. Intense exercise, such as sprinting or running a marathon, can actually reduce your ability to think in the time immediately following these workouts, according to a study conducted by Professor Tomporowski of kinesiology at the University of Georgia. Exercise so rigorous that it causes dehydration or exhaustion may not result in any mental improvement afterward. "Submaximal" exercise for less than sixty minutes is what best boosts your brainpower in the short term.[28]

These findings contradict the macro-resilience perspective, which suggests that a consistent workout schedule gives you all the benefits you need over the long term, *even if you put your routine aside briefly while under pressure*. Focusing on the very short-term research reveals that you won't perform as well if you skip exercise on a day when you need your brain to be in high gear. Micro-resilience underscores the point that the right kind of exercise can aid mental performance right away.

This knowledge has permanently changed what we do daily as an active couple in charge of our own business. Instead of saying, "I am so busy today I can't exercise," both of us make sure we schedule some sort of physical activity—at least a short walk—on the days when our mental performance is critical. Allen loves to block off time to ride his bicycle in the morning before he writes in the afternoon. While on the road for speeches, Bonnie frequents hotel gyms or uses a Tabata timer for interval exercises on the floor of her room. We both feel the positive effects on our writing, speaking, and other high-performance undertakings.

As Wendy Suzuki put it, "When you add exercise into your life, it will give you back more time, more energy, and more productivity."[29]

Exercise Refocus: Tips

1. Make a point of exercising on days when you need your brain to be at its best—for example, when you're giving a speech, writing a proposal, or making a presentation to VIPs. You'll stimulate blood flow, endorphins, and creativity. Instead of saying, "I'm too busy to exercise today," you can say, "I'm so busy today that I must rev up my brain with a little workout."

2. Don't overdo it! Pushing yourself to the point of exhaustion (or exercising for more than sixty minutes) tends to detract from your brainpower, not improve it.

On tough days, do shorter workouts. On more relaxed days, or in the evenings after work, you may want to push harder to build your fitness and health.

3. If you have a meeting with one or two people, conduct a walking meeting through your office campus or around your floor instead of booking a conference room.

4. Develop a suite of exercises you can do right at your desk, including:

   Shoulder rolls: Roll your shoulders forward three to five times, and then roll them backward the same number of times.

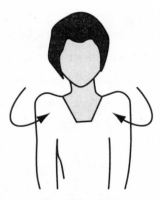

Shoulder Roll

Toe lifts: Raise your toes while keeping your heels firmly on the ground. Hold the stretch for thirty seconds or more. You can also do this while standing.

Toe Lift

Neck stretches: Let your head loll over so that your right ear nearly touches your right shoulder. Using your hand, *gently* press your head a little lower. Hold for ten seconds. Relax and repeat on the other side.

Neck Stretch

The heart opener: Sit on the edge of your chair. Reach behind you and grab the back of the seat with both hands. Inhale and puff out your chest, arching your back. If it's comfortable to do so, let your head fall back slightly to stretch your neck. Continue to breathe and hold the position for thirty seconds or longer.

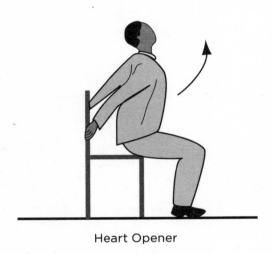

Heart Opener

REFOCUS YOUR BRAIN: CONCLUSION

As humans, we are blessed with a greater capacity than any other species to imagine things that don't exist, to defer instant gratification in service of long-term goals, and to organize our thoughts in complex ways. These executive functions are so valuable and productive that we constantly look for more opportunities to use them to expand our lives.

Yet no one gave us an instruction manual for our brains. As we bombard this precious organ with stimulation, increasing complexity, and more abstraction, we erode its ability to function. Conversely, when we use our brains most efficiently, we raise our performance throughout the day. As we go forward into the future, the ability to improve brain effectiveness will become more and more critical.

Researchers predict that robots and artificial intelligence software will be able to replace many occupations, putting as many as half of the jobs held by American workers at risk.[30] In the legal profession, for example, many paralegal jobs will be taken over by computers that can search through documents much faster and more cheaply. Lawyers who specialize in repetitive transactions, like simple wills, are likely to be replaced by "fill-in-the-blanks" Internet sites. To compete in this new world order and maintain job security, we humans must hone our comparative advantages—our ability to respond to unforeseen circumstances, think critically, and synthesize disparate information. Since refocus techniques permit us to use our prefrontal cortex more efficiently and effectively, they enhance our competitiveness against machines.

Beyond mere survival, refocus strategies offer a better way to live. If we reduce the constant struggle against mental exhaustion, we can replace that exertion with fulfilling impulses like empathy, joy, and creativity. We have the ability to address the challenges we face, envision a better life, set goals for the future, and work toward those goals with grace and ease.

1. John Medina, *Brain Rules: 12 Principles for Surviving and Thriving at Work, Home, and School* (Seattle: Pear Press, 2008).

2. E. K. Miller and J. D. Cohen, "An Integrative Theory of Prefrontal Cortex Function," *Annual Review of Neuroscience* 24 (2001): 167–202; Joaquin M. Fuster, *The Prefrontal Cortex*, 5th ed. (Cambridge: Academic Press, 2015).

3. Donald M. Fisk, "American Labor in the 20th Century," *Compensation and Working Conditions* (Fall 2001).

4. "Goods-Producing Industries," Bureau of Labor Statistics, accessed April 2016, http://www.bls.gov/iag/tgs/iag06.htm.

5. Daniel Kahneman, *Attention and Effort* (Englewood Cliffs, NJ: Prentice Hall, 1973); D. Navon and D. Gopher, "On the Economy of the Human Processing System," *Psychological Review* 86 (1979): 214–255.

6. D. E. Meyer and D. E. Kieras, "A Computational Theory of Executive Cognitive Processes and Multiple-Task Perfor-

mance: Part 1. Basic Mechanisms," *Psychological Review* 104 (1997): 3–65; D. D. Salvucci and N. A. Taatgen, "Threaded Cognition: An Integrated Theory of Concurrent Multitasking," *Psychological Review* 115 (2008): 101–130.

7. "Multitasking: Switching Costs," American Psychological Association, published March 2006, http://www.apa.org/research /action/multitask.aspx.

8. D. L. Strayer, F. A. Drews, and D. J. Crouch, "A Comparison of the Cell Phone Driver and the Drunk Driver," *Human Factors* 48, no. 2 (2006): 381–391.

9. John B. Arden, PhD, *Rewire Your Brain: Think Your Way to a Better Life* (Hoboken, NJ: Wiley, 2010), 70.

10. David Rock, *Your Brain at Work: Strategies for Overcoming Distraction, Regaining Focus, and Working Smarter All Day Long* (New York: HarperCollins, 2009).

11. T. Makany, J. Kemp, and I. E. Dror, "Optimising the Use of Note-Taking as an External Cognitive Aid for Increasing Learning," *British Journal of Educational Technology* 40, no. 4 (2009): 619–635; J. G. Trafton and S. B. Trickett, "Note-Taking for Self-Explanation and Problem Solving," *Human-Computer Interaction* 16, no. 1 (2008): 1–38.

12. I. E. Dror and S. Harnad, "Offloading Cognition onto Cognitive Technology." *Cognition Distributed: How Cognitive Technology Extends Our Minds* 16 (2008): 1–23.

13. John Tierney, "Do You Suffer from Decision Fatigue?" *New York Times Magazine*, August 17, 2011, http://www.nytimes .com/2011/08/21/magazine/do-you-suffer-from-decision -fatigue.html?_r=0.

14. M. Muraven and R. F. Baumeister, "Self-Regulation and Depletion of Limited Resources: Does Self-Control Resemble a Muscle?" *Psychological Bulletin* 126 (2000): 247–259; A. Pocheptsova et al., "Deciding without Resources:

Resource Depletion and Choice in Context," *Journal of Marketing Research* 46 (2009): 344–355; K. D. Vohs et al., "Making Choices Impairs Subsequent Self-Control: A Limited-Resource Account of Decision Making, Self-Regulation, and Active Initiative," *Journal of Personality and Social Psychology* 94 (2008): 883–898.

15. Rachel Kaplan and Stephen Kaplan, *The Experience of Nature: A Psychological Perspective* (Cambridge: Cambridge University Press, 1989).

16. J. M. Tyler and K. C. Burns, "After Depletion: The Replenishment of the Self's Regulatory Resources," *Self and Identity* 7 (2008): 305–321.

17. D. M. Tice et al., "Restoring the Self: Positive Affect Helps Improve Self-Regulation Following Ego Depletion," *Journal of Experimental Social Psychology* 43 (2007): 379–384.

18. M. T. Gailliot and R. F. Baumeister, "The Physiology of Willpower: Linking Blood Glucose to Self-Control," *Personality and Social Psychology Review* 11 (2007): 303–327; M. S. Hagger et al., "Ego Depletion and the Strength Model of Self-Control: A Meta-Analysis," *Psychological Bulletin* 136 (2010): 495–525.

19. Nicholas Bakalar, "Doctors and Decision Fatigue," *Well* (blog), *New York Times*, October 27, 2014, http://well.blogs.nytimes.com/2014/10/27/doctors-and-decision-fatigue/?_r=1; J. A. Linder et al., "Time of Day and Decision to Prescribe Antibiotics," *JAMA Internal Medicine* 174, no. 12 (2014): 2029–2031.

20. Atul Gawande, *The Checklist Manifesto: How to Get Things Right* (New York: Metropolitan Books, 2009), 48.

21. David Rock, *Your Brain at Work: Strategies for Overcoming Distraction, Regaining Focus, and Working Smarter All Day Long* (New York: HarperCollins, 2009), 12.

22. Wendy Suzuki and Billie Fitzpatrick, *Healthy Brain, Happy Life: A Personal Program to Activate Your Brain and Do Everything Better* (New York: HarperCollins, 2015).

23. M. Oppezzo and D. L. Schwartz, "Give Your Ideas Some Legs: The Positive Effect of Walking on Creative Thinking," *Journal of Experimental Psychology: Learning, Memory and Cognition* 40, no. 4 (2014): 1142–1152; Gretchen Reynolds, "Want to Be More Creative? Take a Walk," *Well* (blog), *New York Times*, April 30, 2014, http://well.blogs.nytimes.com/2014/04/30/want-to-be-more-creative-take-a-walk/.

24. J. C. Gondola, "The Effects of a Single Bout of Aerobic Dancing on Selected Tests of Creativity," *Journal of Social Behavior & Personality* 2 (1987): 275–278.

25. John J. Ratey, MD, *A User's Guide to the Brain: Perception, Attention, and the Four Theaters of the Brain* (New York: Pantheon, 2001).

26. K. Lambourne and P. Tomporowski, "The Effect of Exercise-Induced Arousal on Cognitive Task Performance: A Meta-Regression Analysis," *Brain Research* 1341 (2010): 12–24; R. Pennington and S. Hanna, "The Acute Effects of Exercise on Cognitive Performances of Older Adults," *Journal of the Arkansas Academy of Science* 67 (2013): 109–114.

27. H. Steinberg et al., "Exercise Enhances Creativity Independently of Mood," *British Journal of Sports Medicine* 31 (1997): 240–245; D. M. Blanchette et al., "Aerobic Exercise and Creative Potential: Immediate and Residual Effects," *Creativity Research Journal* 17, no. 2–3 (2005): 257–264; Y. Netz et al., "The Effect of a Single Aerobic Training Session on Cognitive Flexibility in Late Middle-Aged Adults," *International Journal of Sports Medicine* 28 (2007): 82–87.

28. P. D. Tomporowski, "Effects of Acute Bouts of Exercise on Cognition," *Acta Psychologica* 112 (2003): 297–324.

29. Wendy Suzuki, "Healthy Brain Happy Life," TEDx video, published December 6, 2014, https://www.youtube.com/watch?v=0cJ5pVtvbZA.

30. Aki Ito, "Your Job Taught to Machines Puts Half U.S. Work at Risk," *Bloomberg*, March 12, 2014, http://www.bloomberg.com/news/articles/2014-03-12/your-job-taught-to-machines-puts-half-u-s-work-at-risk.

3

Reset Your Primitive Alarms

Stop Your Emotions from Being Hijacked

"We must have a pie. Stress cannot exist in the presence of a pie."

—David Mamet

KATHLEEN'S STORY

The scene would seem abhorrent to most people. The short, slightly balding man ranted at the woman sitting behind the ornate partner's desk between them. But to Kathleen, it was just another day at the office.

"How dare you treat me this way?" the angry man railed. "Do you realize the kind of power I have?"

A statuesque blonde woman with soft blue eyes and a warm smile, Dr. Kathleen Cameron is hardly the image one conjures up when thinking of a typical prep-school headmistress. But at the highly esteemed New England prep school where she rules the roost, Kathleen stands first in the line of fire for self-righteous parents like Mr. Angry Man, filled with an exaggerated sense of entitlement after having spent a small fortune in tuition to have Kathleen and her staff educate his children.

> It's really toxic when they go off like that. Sometimes I feel like I have to take a bath or something in order to wash off the whole rotten feeling. But it's an important part of my job to deal with this stuff.

Kathleen desperately needed a way to diffuse the tension and deflect the nearly constant emotional assault—from unhappy parents, disillusioned teachers, an old-guard administration hell-bent on antiquated tradition, and often rebellious Gen Z-ers. After almost ten years behind that large wooden desk, Kathleen felt more like the head *monster* than the headmistress.

All I can do is react. I snap at people, I yell back, I bark orders like a drill sergeant—I hate it. Everything I love about my work seems to have gone right out the window, and I've become a crazy person I don't even recognize.

RESET YOUR PRIMITIVE ALARMS: THE SCIENCE

Kathleen's situation is not terribly unique. Whenever we feel under attack or threatened, or are faced with an emergency, our bodies react strongly and instantaneously in a host of ways that are very difficult to control. Under pressure, we often don't feel quite like ourselves; we do and say things we regret later. "That wasn't me at all," we lament afterward.

The science shows that this "not myself" feeling has

a physical basis. The advanced part of the brain—the PFC—can become hijacked by more primitive parts of the brain, which allows our primal, suspicious, and less intelligent selves to take over. We are *not* our usual selves under intense stress.

The Amygdala Hijack

The amygdala, its name derived from the Greek word for almond, is indeed an almond-shaped mass of gray matter in the front part of each of the temporal lobes of the human cerebral cortex. Part of what the medical field calls the limbic system and sometimes included as part of the older lizard brain, the amygdala plays a key role in responding to what we perceive as threats from the outside world. In Daniel Goleman's seminal book *Emotional Intelligence*, he coined the term "amygdala hijack" to describe emotional responses that are immediate, overwhelming, and out of proportion to the actual stimulus. In the late 1980s, neuroscientist Joseph E. LeDoux uncovered the exact mechanism behind it. Goleman writes:

> **LeDoux discovered a smaller bundle of neurons that leads directly from the thalamus to the**

amygdala, in addition to those going through the larger path of neurons to the cortex. This smaller and shorter pathway—something like a neural back alley—allows the amygdala to receive some direct inputs from the senses and start a response *before* they are fully registered by the neocortex.[1]

Goleman reports that impulses traveling the "back-alley" pathway to a rat's amygdala take only twelve *thousandths* of a second to reach their destination, whereas it takes twice as long for the rat's neocortex to receive the same messages. For humans it's likely that the timing is a bit longer, but the ratio is similar.

If your amygdala senses a threat to your safety, it sounds the alarm and does the equivalent of calling 911 inside your body.[2] Norepinephrine, cortisol, adrenaline, and other fight-or-flight hormones course immediately through your system. Did you ever hear the expression "I'm so mad I can't see straight"? Well, when you're extremely angry, that's literally true. Hormonal boosters narrow your vision, heighten your hearing, increase your heart rate and blood pressure, increase muscle tone, decrease your immune response, cancel attention to any unrelated activities, and launch other physiological reactions to ready your body for fight or flight.

The amygdala hijack greatly increased our chance of survival in the prehistoric world, where quick decisions and reactions to danger were a matter of life and death. Today, however, this fight-or-flight response is often the opposite of the reaction we need for most of our everyday stresses. Instead, higher-order thinking skills such as understanding, analyzing, and creating are required to address twenty-first-century challenges. Once an amygdala hijack occurs, access to our neocortical functions is automatically reduced. We are *less* able to innovate, collaborate, and see the big picture. Under stress, we tend toward negative emotions (e.g., fear, anxiety, anger, pessimism) and are prone to errors in reasoning and analysis. This mismatch between our factory-installed programming for crisis and the reality of the modern world happens all too often.

We will sometimes use the term *emotional hijack* rather than *amygdala hijack* since we cover a wide array of circumstances that may or may not technically involve the amygdala. The amygdala hijack is part of a spectrum that includes the fight-or-flight response as well as other means of threat avoidance.

Prevent the Hijack (or Reduce the Response)

A variety of situations can trigger an emotional hijack. For example, when you are about to give a presentation to a group of senior executives, a major client, or your industry peers, your palms sweat, your heart beats faster, and you feel tongue-tied. Your body's attempt to help you by "keying you up" actually sabotages you.

Lily, a sales rep for a pharmaceutical firm, told us about one morning when her car wouldn't start. Her three-year-old son, Johnny, was already strapped into his car seat in the back. To make matters worse, Lily was supposed to give her husband, Nick, a ride to work that day after they dropped his car off at the dealership for repairs. As she and Nick desperately searched for jumper cables in the trunk, the possibility that Lily might miss her 9:30 meeting with a prospective client loomed large.

This kind of scenario kicks off a chain reaction in your body that makes you feel like a locomotive leaving the station—the pistons pound faster, the wheels churn, the steam pours out, and soon the momentum of a heavy freight train of emotions feels unstoppable.

Yet once we become aware of the process, we can take steps to either avert the hijack or at least put some brakes on the train. Since Lily had been through our Micro-Resilience training, she quickly recognized what was going on and used the tools to turn herself around. While her husband jump-started the car, she took an opportunity to enjoy a little extra time with Johnny, who was fascinated by the whole process. She dropped off both of them and still made it to her meeting on time. Micro-resilience may not have been the reason she made it to her meeting, but it did reduce the mental and physical toll during the process.

Unfortunately, these types of emotional reactions are common in the workplace. Daniel Goleman has identified the five most likely triggers of an office hijack:[3]

1. Condescension and disrespect

2. Unfair treatment

3. Lack of appreciation

4. Feeling you aren't listened to or heard

5. Unrealistic deadlines and demands

For example, if you weren't invited to a dinner meeting or included on a certain project team, you might feel threatened to a degree that's out of proportion to the actual events. Experiments using functional magnetic resonance imaging (fMRI) brain scans to monitor a simulation of being left out in a playground ball-tossing game show that exclusion ignites the same kind of brain activity as physical pain.[4] We may have evolved to experience rejection as pain because connection to a group may have meant the difference between life and death in primitive cultures.[5] A small social slight—something as innocuous as the placement of a desk in a new office space—can feel like a life-threatening issue.

Scientists have also shown that worry about the stress in our lives can cause as much damage as the stress itself.[6] Kelly McGonigal, a Stanford University psychologist, made exactly this point in her legendary TED talk, "How to Make Stress Your Friend."[7] Stress isn't only what happens to us; it is how we react. Understanding that the emotional hijack is designed to help us—and that we can moderate the effects when they aren't necessary—means that the stressors that assault us in life have less destructive power.

Awfulizing: Hijacked for No Reason

Not every threat we perceive and react to actually harms us; the threat may not even have existed in the first place. Psychologists use the words *awfulizing* and *catastrophizing* to describe the tendency we have to imagine the worst possible scenarios.[8] For example, if the boss frowns as she walks by your desk without saying hello, you can easily invent reasons for her behavior: my last report had mistakes; she doesn't like me; something happened with my biggest client; and so on. You create a scenario in which your job is at risk, you won't be able to pay your mortgage, your daughter will have to leave college because you can't afford the tuition, and you'll get divorced... but most often, you subsequently find there was a perfectly understandable explanation for your boss's actions that had nothing to do with you. Maybe she was distracted because of a fender bender she had on the way back from her lunch meeting.

All this worry takes an excruciating toll on your energy, focus, and health. Stress hormones—which suppress your immune system, tense your muscles, and put you on edge—take a long time to dissipate. In the meantime, you suffer the physical and cognitive drains of dealing with a crisis *that never existed in the first place.*

Research specifically designed to test resilience in regard to awfulizing found that "resilient people flexibly and appropriately adjust the level of emotional resources needed to meet the demands of the situation."[9] Resilient people are able to scrape themselves off the ceiling much faster when they realize that danger will not materialize after all. Other people, however, continue to show chemical and physical indicators of stress long after the threat dissipates.

This seems to be as true of high achievers who pressure themselves to succeed as it is for stay-at-home parents who fret about the health and happiness of family members, community issues, and every other aspect of "holding it all together." As Mark Twain said, "I've seen a heap of trouble in my life, and most of it never came to pass."

RESET YOUR PRIMITIVE ALARMS: SOLUTIONS

Damage from the repeated triggering of our fight-or-flight hormones is not inevitable. By regularly pushing back on our vestigial alarm system, we can rewire our neural and physical responses so that they are more aligned with our current, complex reality.

Labeling Reset: Call It by Name

Back at the New England prep school, we asked headmistress Kathleen to put labels on her feelings during confrontations with parents and teachers. Was she angry? Frustrated? Did she feel vulnerable? Ashamed? Scientists have demonstrated that we can distance ourselves from a feeling when we simply come up with a name for it. Recent fMRI studies conducted by Matthew Lieberman and his team at UCLA have shown that labeling disrupts the threat response by increasing activity in the prefrontal cortex.[10] Instead of being consumed by our reactions, we can scrutinize them as an impartial observer.

A phrase such as *I'm angry* or *I'm feeling cornered* can help you put the brakes on your emotional locomotive. Once you separate yourself from a feeling and stimulate your thought processes—once you reset your primitive alarm system—you realize you have the power to choose a different emotional response, such as compassion, humor, or commitment.[11] Dr. Daniel Amen, a leading authority on brain-scanning techniques, agrees. "Often, just naming the thought can help take away its power," says Dr. Amen.[12] When you find yourself endlessly running hypothetical doomsday scenarios, for example, call it what it is: say to yourself, "I'm awfulizing" or "I'm catastrophizing." Labeling can put you back on track and restore some of the energy your emotions have hijacked.

When she tried labeling, Kathleen noticed that it increased her sense of control. Now, unbeknownst to her guests, Kathleen's notes during confrontational meetings cover not only action steps and follow-up items but also descriptions of her emotions during each encounter. The process gives her more power to separate herself from her emotions.

Labeling Reset: Tips

1. When a rising tide of emotions threatens to take you off course, stop and put a label (or several) on what you are feeling. You can do this (silently) during a meeting, when you are about to give a speech, or when provoked by a coworker. Name your feelings, and you'll loosen their emotional grip at once.

2. Remember that you have choices about how you behave, and the way you behave can in turn influence the way you feel. If a coworker is rude, you can be angry, or you can choose to react with compassion. You can be rude, too, or you can simply ignore her. You can give her the silent treatment, or you can make a joke.

3. After you've labeled a negative emotion, rename it and give it a new, positive label. If you feel anxious or nervous before a presentation, for example, you can relabel the emotion "excitement" or "a feeling of intense caring."

Conscious Relaxation Reset: Interrupt the Stress Response

Early one morning during our preparation for a full-day leadership program at a Fortune 100 health-care company, one of the participants, Marion, arrived distraught. While she was still in her hotel room that morning, her husband had called her from their home, across the country, to tell her that their son had broken his arm and was headed to the emergency room. The combination of shock and fear made her so agitated that she dropped her phone in the toilet. She arrived early for our seminar but looked visibly shaken. We suggested that Marion take a deep breath—but as she did so, we watched her shoulders move up and down and her chest heave. We immediately stopped her and showed her a better way to slow her adrenaline rush.

Although taking a deep breath when you're under stress is widely given advice, it's much less well known that breathing from your chest, as Marion did, can actually make things worse. Fear and anger trigger shallow breathing, high in the chest, which provides between eight and ten times *less* air volume than using your diaphragm to take deep abdominal breaths. Chest breathing requires far more work than diaphragmatic breathing, and as a result chest breathing can actually increase your stress level.[13] "Shifting from constricted breathing to relaxed, natural breathing turns off the body's fight-or-flight stress response. This balances the autonomic nervous system and produces a feeling of relaxed energy, mental clarity, and a physiological state that promotes health and vitality," according to researchers.[14]

Dr. Daniel Amen confesses that deep-belly breathing has been one of the most helpful exercises he's ever done:

> When I first learned how to breathe diaphragmatically, I discovered that my baseline breathing rate was twenty-four breaths a minute and I breathed mostly with my upper chest. I had spent ten years in the military, taught to stick my chest out and suck my gut in (the opposite of what is good for breathing). Quickly I learned how to quiet my breathing and help it be more efficient. Not only did it help my feelings of anxiety, it also helped me feel more settled overall. I still use it to calm my nerves before tough meetings, speaking engagements, and media appearances. I also use it, in conjunction with self-hypnosis, to help me sleep when I feel stressed. My current baseline breathing rate is less than ten times a minute.[15]

We found this to be extremely helpful for Kathleen, the school headmistress. She was well accustomed to belly-breathing techniques because she is a trained jazz singer. But she didn't realize she could use them in conjunction with deliberate muscle relaxation (see tip 2 that follows) to purge tension during high-intensity episodes. After a few weeks of experimentation, Kathleen decided on a ritual of deep breathing and relaxation exercises at regular intervals throughout her day, and she made it a point to add extra sessions when she knew a big blast of negativity was on its way.

This technique is truly micro in scale. Once you get the hang of it, you can use it in all kinds of highly stressful situations—and no one will be able to realize you're doing it. Consciously relax for one minute, five minutes, or as long as you need. Just a few deep breaths before you walk into someone's office can downshift your limbic system and make all the difference to the outcome of your meeting.

In addition to using this technique in a crisis moment, you can set reminders to consciously relax several times a day. This will help you respond in a manageable way to the many small things that build tension: you were cut off in traffic on the way to work; you spilled coffee on your notes; an important client postponed a meeting. Each little thing causes your neck and shoulders to tense up a tiny bit more, creating cumulative, yet quite unnecessary, muscle fatigue. A minute or two of conscious relaxation and deep breathing between appointments works for nonathletes just as it works for tennis champions who recover between points. If you don't have *any* time between calls and meetings, you can perform conscious relaxation techniques while you talk on the phone, walk down the hall, or sit in a conference room. No matter how crazy your schedule is, you can build this reset into your day.

Conscious Relaxation Reset: Tips

1. For most of us, it takes time and practice to strengthen the long-unused diaphragm muscles that are essential for deep-belly breathing. Get started by practicing these simple steps:

    Sit down: Make sure you're in a comfortable place, with your feet on the floor.

    Center yourself: Put your hand on your abdomen, just over your navel.

    Exhale: Let all the air out of your body with a big sigh and relax.

    Inhale: As you breathe back in, expand your belly so it pushes your hand outward.

    Repeat: Take a few more breaths slowly in and out. Focus all the breathing movement in your belly

while you keep your shoulders and chest relaxed
and quiet.

2. Deliberately relax your muscles as you do the deep
breathing:

Release your shoulders: Start with deep abdominal
breathing. After several breaths, release your
shoulders as you breathe out.
Give in to gravity: On the next breath, let gravity
relax your shoulders even further.
Focus on individual muscles: Repeat this process
from head to toe—neck, arms, legs, and so on.
Allow the tension to flow down toward the floor
and out through your toes. Feel the deep relaxation with each breath.
Finish with a breath: Inhale and exhale one more
time, and pay attention to how relaxed you are.
Maintain that feeling as you turn your attention
back to work.

3. Enhance the abdominal breathing and muscle relaxation with positive thoughts by concentrating on
things you are grateful for, or by thinking of the people who love you. This will increase parasympathetic

activity and help stop or reverse the fight-or-flight chain reaction.[16] Positive mental and emotional states align respiration and heart variability into a synchronized and efficient pattern called "heart rhythm coherence."[17] This cardiac coherence improves cognitive performance[18] and boosts the immune system.[19] A combination of deep breathing and positive feelings can improve hormonal balance (resulting in reduced cortisol and higher levels of DHEA) and lower stress, anxiety, burnout, and feelings of guilt.[20]

Sensory Reset: Use "Smells and Bells"

Bonnie first saw Dr. Joan Borysenko speak at a large convention in Texas. Over the course of her remarkable career, Joan has taught at Harvard Medical School, pioneered the study of integrative medicine, cofounded a mind-body clinic with Dr. Herbert Benson, and authored breakthrough books such as *Minding the Body, Mending the Mind*. Yet it was her personal story and courage that most mesmerized Bonnie.

Joan was a postdoctoral candidate in cancer-cell biology at Harvard when her father was diagnosed with stage IV cancer. She tearfully described the day he died—not from cancer but from leaping out a hospital

window. The disease, the medication, and the pain con-
spired to affect his mental state to such an extent that
he took his own life. Joan explained how this devastating turn of events changed the course of her career
and propelled her to study behavioral medicine and
psychoneuroimmunology.

When we began to research our Micro-Resilience
program, Bonnie called Joan to ask for advice. While
Joan's published writings relate to several of the topics in
our Five Frameworks—breathing, positive emotions, and
resilience in general—there was one brand-new nugget
Joan shared in that phone conversation: "Certain scents
can cut right through an emotional hijack," she said.
"For example, cinnamon, vanilla, and nutmeg."[21]

"Is that because they remind us of the holidays?"
Bonnie asked.

Joan explained that it is the other way around. These
scents have the power to deescalate our limbic reactions
and relax us. That's why they have become associated
with holidays.

Dr. Daniel Amen corroborates Joan's statement in his
book *Change Your Brain, Change Your Life*: "Because
your sense of smell goes directly to the deep limbic system, it is easy to see why smells can have such a powerful impact on our feeling states. The right smells likely
cool the deep limbic system. Pleasing fragrances are

like an anti-inflammatory. By surrounding yourself with flowers, sweet fragrances, and other pleasant smells, you affect the working of your brain in a powerful and positive way."[22]

We remembered Kathleen's telling us that the smell of spearmint brought back pleasant memories of her mother brewing tea with the fresh mint leaves that grew in the woods behind her home. We suggested that she keep a supply of mint tea bags in her office to re-create the aroma whenever she felt the need for it. After a few weeks she reported an additional discovery: Wint O Green Life Savers have exactly the same scent as her mom's tea and also soothe her frayed nerves. The candy probably works both chemically and nostalgically. That is, a hijack starts because your brain receives sensory input that aligns with the memory of a threat, setting off your primitive alarms. Conversely, sensory input that aligns with deeply *positive, safe* memories slows down the panic reaction.[23] Kathleen placed a big bag of Wint O Greens in her desk drawer, where she can grab one anytime her blood pressure starts to rise.

Not surprisingly, Kathleen came up with another way to dissolve the tension in difficult conversations:

I got into the habit of asking parents if they would like a drink from the café we have on

campus. We'll take a walk down there, get a coffee, and then stroll back to my office. And all the while they're looking at the amazing facility we have here—kids laughing and running around, having a great time—and the overall ambience of our beautiful school. You would think I had lassoed the moon. They become so grateful and so stunned—it just completely changes the tone of the conversation.

But then she told us about something that really blew our minds. Kathleen turned her whole office into one big reset for her primitive alarms.

I had a pair of hard, dark chairs in my office that are the most uncomfortable things in the world. It just made me miserable to sit in them. I also had a huge Currier & Ives print on the wall that portrayed armed men on horseback charging after a poor little fox, scared out of its mind. What kind of message does that send? So I redecorated the walls with photographs of beaches and sunsets. I replaced the torturous chairs with a comfy sofa and two soft upholstered chairs. I also have a beautiful tropical fish tank that some graduating seniors gave to me on the last day of school. I absolutely love it! Just hearing the filter gurgling is incredibly soothing. And there's one crazy fish that picks up pieces of coral and tosses them at the glass to clean its "house." Sometimes in the middle of an intense conversation, I hear *plink, plink, plink*—and it's all I can do to keep from laughing out loud! Even if I'm not having an enjoyable conversation, I'm surrounded by beautiful things I love, and it feels like home. If I've invited a stranger in, I'm not going to allow him to bother me, because I could kick him out at any point. I know I'm in my office and that my visitors—including difficult parents—pay my salary, but this new outlook really makes a difference in how I handle things.

Dr. Borysenko also explained that some sounds can cut through the amygdala response as well as smells, which may account for the soothing benefits from Kathleen's fish tank plinks and gurgles. We saw the effect of sound in practice when we researched our book *How Great Women Lead* and visited the home of fashion industry CEO Eileen Fisher to observe a meeting she hosted for all her senior executives. To begin the meeting, Eileen turned to a woman in the circle and asked:

"Susan, would you lead us in a moment of silence?"

Susan nodded a peaceful assent and stepped up to a small table just inside the circle that held a Chinese brass bowl on a silk pillow. She smiled at everyone, picked up a short, thick wooden stick, and tapped once on the bowl. The vibrating chime radiated a serene wave of sound so powerful I felt it deep in my bones. My breathing slowed once again. My nerves relaxed. I melted into the gentle stillness that seeped into the room like water flowing into every nook and cranny.

Although this practice seems too "new age" to be used in most corporate settings, the science behind it underscores its effectiveness. By calming the participants' stress responses, the pure tone helps clear away things they might be worrying about, dials back the negative effects of limbic arousal, and at the same time increases their access to their advanced brain resources. This unusual way to start a business meeting enhances every participant's ability to collaborate, to avoid pessimism, and be more open to finding innovative solutions.

Sensory Reset: Tips

1. Experiment with various scents to find out what works best for you. Lavender or eucalyptus? Lemon or almond? Buy scented candles, room spray, or potpourri in that scent and keep it in strategic places around your work space. Be sensitive to those around you, though, who may have allergies or dislike strong perfumes.

2. Find portable means of keeping soothing aromas handy. Tic Tacs, gum, hand lotion, and herbal teas are just a few examples. Some people put a drop of essential oil in their palm and inhale the pure scent.

3. Choose a playlist of favorite music that puts you in a positive frame of mind. A song you remember from your teenage years, perhaps? A slow, soft instrumental solo or string quartet? Pleasant music calms your aroused state by stimulating your prefrontal cortex.[24] If playing music aloud isn't an option, load these pieces into your smartphone or MP3 player and play them through headphones when the going gets tough.

4. Kick off meetings large and small with a resonant bell, lively music, or another choice that works for your culture. When speakers begin with a joke, cascades of laughter can also achieve a "palate-cleansing" effect.

Power Pose Reset: Reduce Fear and Boost Confidence

Harvard Business School professor Amy Cuddy, author of *Presence* (based on her TED talk about "power poses" and the way our body language shapes who we are—a talk that has been viewed more than thirty-two million times), offers another technique for quickly and easily preventing or deescalating our hijacks. She noticed that female students in her class were getting lower grades than the male students, and she hypothesized that this was because nonverbal behavior is such an important part of her evaluation: 50 percent of a student's grade is based on class participation. She then became interested in whether nonverbal behavior can affect our inner selves as much as it affects the way others perceive us and treat us. And sure enough, if we *act* confident and powerful, Amy discovered, we *become* more confident and powerful.

Based on the observation that animals in the wild— from cobras to primates to peacocks—use open and expansive poses to express dominance, Cuddy and her colleagues posed forty-two people in either submissive or dominant poses. The people in submissive poses were physically closed and contracted, almost rolled up in a ball. The people in dominant poses were physically open: they had their feet spread apart and their hands on their hips.

The researchers found significant increases in testosterone and reductions in cortisol, a hormone associated with fear and stress, in the "dominant" group. Participants who struck poses of power also felt more comfortable taking risks in return for a chance at receiving a reward at the end of the experiment.[25]

When an emotional hijack occurs because we feel threatened, stressed, or helpless, simply striking a powerful pose—keeping our arms held out from our sides or leaning forward on our desks—can make us feel stronger and less afraid. This shape-shift may send an internal signal that we are still in control and may also lower our levels of cortisol and other fear-related hormones.

Power Pose Reset: Tips

1. Experiment with your body language—preferably in front of a mirror: Stand with your legs apart and your hands on your hips. Try reclining in a chair with your feet up on a desk and your hands clasped behind your head.

Those poses take up space and are open. Now try sitting down with your hands in your lap, shoulders hunched over, and head down. That's contracted and closed. Notice how you feel in each position.

2. Before predictably stressful situations, such as presentations, speeches, or large meetings, close the door to your office or go to another private place where you can practice striking a power pose. Use what you practiced when you step in front of the group. When you feel threatened by disrespectful behavior from a coworker or fearful because you've received bad news from a client, try to maintain open and expansive postures that will support your strength and confidence. Look up Cuddy's TED talk to clarify what power poses look like and how to use them.

RESET YOUR PRIMITIVE ALARMS: CONCLUSION

Emotional hijacks are survival mechanisms held over from primitive times, when most threats required physical rather than intellectual responses. But in today's world, these physical responses are the opposite of what we really need. We solve our modern problems more effectively by using brainpower and sophisticated levels of emotional intelligence than by reacting in a narrow-minded, impulsive way. The good news is that we can rewire ourselves and essentially upgrade our human operating system to cope with the challenges we face. One of the most exciting developments in recent brain science is the discovery that our brains are much more malleable than we thought. With practice and attention, we can retrain ourselves to be more effective and to waste less energy on outdated responses to reality.

The damage from *not* choosing to reset our primitive alarms can be enormous. In moments when our personality is hijacked and we lose control of our emotions, we risk permanent damage to our relationships with friends, loved ones, bosses, and clients. Conversely, people who seldom blow up but rather internalize all their frustration, anger, and fear also run into problems. Although holding your emotions in may seem like a practical and nondestructive way to behave, the buildup of internalized negative feelings can lead to less-than-optimal performance, serious health issues, and a diminished ability to enjoy life. The more often a hijack sets off panic alarms, the more cortisol, adrenaline, and other stress hormones wash through your body. Chronic anxiety can interfere with your immune system, your body's ability to rest and digest, and other essential functions. Whether you blow up at other people or suppress your feelings, you pay a high price for allowing your amygdala to run around without a leash.

We do not suggest that all emotional hijacks should be eliminated. When you walk through an unsafe area, wake up to a fire in your home, or react to avoid a deer on the freeway, your adrenal response is vital. Anger, fear, and other emotions can be legitimate reactions to life's twists and turns. In some cases, though, when you reset your primitive alarms, you are better able to hear what these feelings are trying to tell you:

- The labeling reset helps you validate your feelings without being controlled by them

- The conscious relaxation reset helps you prevent blowups before they occur

- The sensory reset helps keep you in a calm frame of mind

- The power pose reset helps keep you in control— the *real* you, not the one who feels cornered and threatened

Once your internal alarms are managed, you may still become outraged in specific ways and at specific times. But your reactions will feel more like a choice—they will feel conscious rather than instinctive. As Aristotle said, "Anyone can become angry, that is easy...; but to be angry with the right person, to the right degree, at the right time, for the right purpose, and in the right way— that is not easy." These methods aren't designed to eliminate your emotions; they just help prevent you from losing your mind when you express them.

1. Daniel Goleman, *Emotional Intelligence: Why It Can Matter More than IQ* (New York: Bantam Books, 2006).
2. John J. Ratey, MD, *A User's Guide to the Brain: Perception, Attention, and the Four Theaters of the Brain* (New York: Pantheon, 2001).
3. Daniel Goleman, "Emotional Mastery," *Leadership Excellence* 28, no. 6 (2011): 12–13.
4. N. I. Eisenberger, M. D. Lieberman, and K. D. Williams, "Does Rejection Hurt? An fMRI Study of Social Exclusion," *Science* 302 (2003): 290–292.
5. E. E. Nelson and J. Panksepp, "Brain Substrates of Infant-Mother Attachment: Contributions of Opioids, Oxytocin, and Norepinephrine," *Neuroscience and Biobehavioral Reviews* 22, no. 3 (1998): 437–452.
6. A. Keller et al., "Does the Perception That Stress Affects Health Matter? The Association with Health and Mortality," *Health Psychology* 31, no. 5 (2012): 677; J. P. Jamieson, M. K. Nock, and W. B. Mendes, "Mind over Matter: Reappraising Arousal Improves Cardiovascular and Cognitive Responses to Stress," *Journal of Experimental Psychology: General* 141.3 (2012): 417.
7. Kelly McGonigal, "How to Make Stress Your Friend," TED

video, published June 2013, https://www.ted.com/talks/kelly _mcgonigal_how_to_make_stress_your_friend?language=en.

8. Joan Borysenko, PhD, *Minding the Body, Mending the Mind* (Cambridge: Da Capo Press, 2007).

9. C. E. Waugh et al., "The Neural Correlates of Trait Resilience When Anticipating and Recovering from Threat," *Social Cognitive and Affective Neuroscience* Advance Access (September 2, 2008) doi: 10.1093/scan/nsn024.

10. M. D. Lieberman et al., "Putting Feelings into Words: Affect Labeling Disrupts Amygdala Activity in Response to Affective Stimuli," *Psychological Science* 18, no. 5 (2007): 421–428.

11. John B. Arden, PhD, *Rewire Your Brain: Think Your Way to a Better Life* (Hoboken, NJ: Wiley, 2010), 26.

12. Daniel G. Amen, MD, *Change Your Brain, Change Your Life: The Breakthrough Program for Conquering Anxiety, Depression, Obsessiveness, Lack of Focus, Anger, and Memory Problems* (New York: Harmony, 2015), 156.

13. Joan Borysenko, PhD, *Minding the Body, Mending the Mind* (Cambridge: Da Capo Press, 2007); Jeffrey Rossman, PhD, *The Mind-Body Mood Solution: The Breakthrough Drug-Free Program for Lasting Relief from Depression* (Emmaus, PA: Rodale, 2010), 101.

14. Jeffrey Rossman, PhD, *The Mind-Body Mood Solution: The Breakthrough Drug-Free Program for Lasting Relief from Depression* (Emmaus, PA: Rodale, 2010), 101.

15. Daniel G. Amen, MD, *Change Your Brain, Change Your Life: The Breakthrough Program for Conquering Anxiety, Depression, Obsessiveness, Lack of Focus, Anger, and Memory Problems* (New York: Harmony, 2015), 152.

16. R. McCraty et al., "The Effects of Emotions on Short-Term Power Spectral Analysis of Heart Rate Variability," *American Journal of Cardiology* 76, no. 14 (1995): 1089–1093.

17. W. A. Tiller, R. McCraty, and M. Atkinson, "Cardiac Coherence: A New, Noninvasive Measure of Autonomic Nervous System Order," *Alternative Therapies in Health and Medicine* 2, no. 1 (1996): 52–65.

18. "Cardiac Coherence Improves Cognitive Performance: Influence of Afferent Cardiovascular Input on Cognitive Performance and Alpha Activity," *Proceedings of the Annual Meeting of the Pavlovian Society,* Rollin McCraty and Mike Atkinson (Tarrytown, NY, 1999).

19. G. Rein, M. Atkinson, and R. McCraty, "The Physiological and Psychological Effects of Compassion and Anger," *Journal of Advancement in Medicine* 8, no. 2 (1995): 87–105.

20. R. McCraty et al., "The Impact of a New Emotional Self-Management Program on Stress, Emotions, Heart-Rate Variability, DHEA and Cortisol," *Integrative Physiological and Behavioral Science* 33, no. 2 (1998): 151–170.

21. Joan Borysenko, in discussion with the author, 2011.

22. Daniel G. Amen, MD, *Change Your Brain, Change Your Life: The Breakthrough Program for Conquering Anxiety, Depression, Obsessiveness, Lack of Focus, Anger, and Memory Problems* (New York: Harmony, 2015), 93.

23. John Medina, *Brain Rules: 12 Principles for Surviving and Thriving at Work, Home, and School* (Seattle: Pear Press, 2008).

24. D. Soto et al., "Pleasant Music Overcomes the Loss of Awareness in Patients with Visual Neglect," *Proceedings of the National Academy of Sciences of the United States of America* 106, no. 14 (2009): 6011–6016, doi: 10.1073/pnas.0811681106.

25. D. R. Carney, A. J. C. Cuddy, and A. J. Yap, "Power Posing: Brief Nonverbal Displays Affect Neuroendocrine Levels and Risk Tolerance," *Psychological Science* 21, no. 10 (October 2010): 1363–1368.

4

Reframe Your Attitude

Spiral into the Positive

"Optimism is the faith that leads to achievement; nothing can be done without hope."

—Helen Keller

Priya's Story

Though her luxury hotel lay along one of the most scenic canals in Amsterdam, Priya felt none of the majesty of "the Venice of the North." She'd been on the road almost constantly for more than four months, and the isolation of her nomadic existence was depleting her. Every day, after her regular breakfast of an egg-white omelet and herbal tea, she went straight to work and stayed there all day long. Work, sleep; work, sleep. Priya was tethered to the treadmill of a high-powered global executive.

Many people would crumble under this kind of pressure, but Priya, a fast-track leader at an international biotech firm, seemed to thrive on it. Exceptional performance, international travel, and long hours were expected from her and everyone around her. She pushed her people hard—and pushed herself even harder— which fed her reputation as a slave driver.

People say I'm too direct, too aggressive, with no empathy or compassion. But at the end of the day I still have to run a business. I can't just kowtow to people all the time and say everything

is rosy. Plus, I like to be in control. If I don't get my way, I get very upset and negative. This is an issue for me personally and professionally.

This classic type A existence earned Priya a great deal of success, but was, in the process, taking a tremendous toll on her health. She began to lose her hair as a result of the stress; her blood pressure crept up, and her doctor became concerned. Friends begged her to sit still and "chill out" from time to time.

But I have so much on my plate. If I take any time during the day to stop and relax I feel horrible, almost as if I had wasted money.

And Priya's career wasn't the only thing hanging in the balance. Her voice cracked as she became even more personal with us.

I grew up in a very traditional culture where women marry young and start a family. I have always wanted a family, but I want a career, too. Not being married at age thirty-six makes me very tense. That tension makes it impossible for me to be relaxed enough to date anyone. This

tension spills over into my work, and the stress of work undermines my personal life in turn.

Priya had been working diligently to improve her leadership style for more than a year and was disappointed with her progress. She had recently received another round of feedback that showed virtually no improvement over the last twelve months: her left-brain, quantitative style lacked empathy; she didn't connect well in a social context. She explained:

> I call and check in to find out whether my team members are overwhelmed on a project overseas. I take people out for coffee. I tell them to use the car service late at night instead of driving. I tell them to take clients out for a nice meal and find other ways to enjoy themselves. I have also tried to get them to tell me what I should be doing differently—but I don't get concrete answers. I try to let them know I care about them and that I am working on these things with a coach. I even saw an image consultant who told me I would seem more approachable if I don't cross my arms when talking to others and smile more. I feel as though I am making a huge effort; it is

very frustrating to be told I haven't gotten better. I feel lost. I feel vulnerable.

The source of negativity for Priya was a baseline of troubling thoughts and feelings that pervaded her daily life. No matter how hard she tried to mimic the behavior of an upbeat and empathetic leader, the underlying harshness of her attitude toward herself and others overshadowed everything else.

REFRAME YOUR ATTITUDE: THE SCIENCE

Any of us can easily become mired in a negativity rut. We can't help it: our physiology is designed to draw us strongly and quickly toward apprehension, rage, or pessimism whenever we feel threatened. It's evolutionary: our prehistoric ancestors developed rapid and intense reactions to negative, or even potentially negative, stimuli because such responses were a matter of life and death.[1] Positive stimuli, on the other hand, didn't require early humans to expend so much energy. As a result, we have inherited a slow, diffuse, almost lackadaisical response to the good things in life[2] while maintaining a furious intensity about the bad.

The fact that we evolved, for survival purposes, to be more negative than positive largely explains why we quickly spiral downward into suspicion, fear, and anger in response to negative situations. The lizard brain inside us still reacts as if life were nasty, brutish, and short. It doesn't know the world has changed.

To stay positive, see possibilities, and commit to our values more than our impulses, we have to train ourselves to react differently from our primal predecessors. We have to slow the negative spiral and amplify the positive and advanced aspects of our minds. To borrow from the motto of the Olympics—*Citius, Altius, Fortius*—we have to develop a faster, higher, and stronger positive response to life.

The Benefits of Positivity

Research across numerous fields links positivity and optimism with more earning power, better health, greater longevity, and more satisfying relationships. Optimistic life insurance agents sold 88 percent more than their pessimistic counterparts, according to one of more than six hundred studies on this subject by psychologist Martin Seligman.[3] Whereas traditional psychology focuses on pathology, Seligman, a self-confessed pessimist, pioneered research into positive psychology. Michele Phillips, author of *Happiness Is a Habit*, summed up the results of this research with this phrase: "Pessimists may be right more often, but optimists are more successful."[4]

When you think positively, you broaden your visual attention, stimulate your immune system, and execute with more precision.[5] Experiments have also linked an uptick in positive emotions to closeness with others, improved trust, and cross-racial affinity.[6] Better performance at work comes along with this as well. Increased positivity leads to creativity,[7] openness to new experiences,[8] and a good attitude toward critical feedback.[9] Optimism also lowers the health risks traditionally associated with type A overachievers.[10]

It may seem surprising that something as ephemeral as "good feelings" can shift the entire trajectory of our lives. The broaden-and-build theory of positive emotions, developed by Dr. Barbara Fredrickson, psychology professor at the University of North Carolina at Chapel Hill, suggests that although upbeat emotions broaden our thoughts and actions only temporarily, they allow us to build up durable resources. Moments of positive feeling, when frequently repeated, can build effective relationships and interpersonal networks. Similarly, openness and creativity at work support skill development and knowledge acquisition that can set you apart from others. "Positive emotions expand people's mindsets in ways that, little-by-little, reshape who they are."[11]

Fredrickson goes on to demonstrate through meticulous tests that we can increase our daily average of positive emotions by choosing thoughts and creating habits that support higher levels of positivity. In prior research, it had been assumed that repeated, external stimuli were needed to engender increased positive feelings in study participants. One of Fredrickson's breakthroughs was to prove that individuals can self-generate sustainable and significant improvements.[12]

Another realm of research, positive organizational behavior, goes beyond the individual to quantify the impact of positivity on companies and teams. Leaders who develop positive business climates, relationships, and communications often achieve results that exceed expectations by spectacular margins.[13] An increasing amount of research into the workplace environment shows that a positive attitude and optimism lead to increased employee engagement, better performance, and less turnover.[14]

REFRAME YOUR ATTITUDE: SOLUTIONS

If the thought of developing a positive attitude as a solution to your problems seems too easy, touchy-feely, or insubstantial, don't let the simplicity of it fool you: this process requires hard work and the payoff is enormous. The techniques that follow are based on voluminous research that ties positivity to practical, real-world outcomes.

Joy Kit Reframe: Apply First Aid to Your Emotional Cuts and Bruises

Picture a typical first-aid kit—a white plastic or metal box about the size of a lunch box, painted with a red cross on the front. We keep these kits at home because we know that eventually someone will get a cut or burn that requires treatment. That was our original inspiration for the Joy Kit: no matter how hard we try to maintain it, our positive attitude will, from time to time, get burned or cut or injured in some way, so why not be ready with a first-aid kit for joy? When clients overreact, deadlines seem impossible, or coworkers don't give you what you need to meet your commitments, you can access your personal stash of things guaranteed to cheer you up.

Priya explained how well the Joy Kit works for her:

I keep a file on my computer called Happiness. It contains thank-you notes, e-mails from my nephews, and cards from friends, family, and even coworkers. I can change my perspective quickly by pulling up this file and looking at it for even a minute or two. I have even added my iPhone to my virtual Joy Kit. I look at pictures that have positive associations and positive text

messages when I am stuck waiting for a cab or hung up in an airport somewhere.

After six weeks in our program using an array of micro-resilience strategies, Priya began to see big changes.

My friends say my energy is softer, more open and positive. Several different people have commented on it. And...I am finally actually dating someone!

This revelation really touched our hearts. True to form, Priya didn't gush about her romance. But it was clear she was thrilled with this development. Her new-found positivity set in motion a sea change in her interactions with everyone—friends, family, clients, and coworkers. Everything she'd done to try to make her teams *think* she was nicer and more positive paled in comparison to who she became after this work truly set in. We'd never expected that micro-resilience would lead to love, but we were thrilled when it did!

What shifts us to the positive is unique to each individual, so your Joy Kit should be completely personal. Bonnie's consists of a miniature red canvas tote bag that contains chocolate, a picture of her daughter when she was a toddler, and a note from her (departed) mother in her extravagant, old-fashioned penmanship that says, "Cherish yourself." Allen has a bag full of IOUs from his youngest daughter promising hugs and kisses, pictures of sailboats and ski mountains, and a small painting his older daughter gave him when she was little. We've seen people include bottles of sand from vacations in Aruba and Acapulco. Others keep digital recordings of their dogs barking or their children laughing. Thank-you notes you've received can help when it seems as if no one appreciates you. If you stop for a few minutes to contemplate what brings you from "down in the dumps" to "up and at 'em," you can take better charge of how you feel.

Joy Kit Reframe: Tips

1. Make a list of things that inspire joy in you—photos, souvenirs, mementos, music, poems, thank-you notes, and other items.

2. Keep joy-inspiring items handy in a bag or a box on your desk. When you experience a down moment, take one or two of these items out and focus on them. Items you view on your desk every day, like family photos, may not pack the same punch as something you draw on only when you need a lift.

3. Create a digital Joy Kit—a folder on your computer, tablet, or phone that contains articles, songs, and pictures that make you feel good. Priya's iPhone Joy Kit travels everywhere with her.

4. Ask someone at work or in your family to surprise you with something from your Joy Kit when you are having a bad day. We're often the last people to know when we need it ourselves.

5. If you know someone well, you can make a "starter" Joy Kit as a gift. Fill it with the recipient's favorite foods, photos of shared memories, or perhaps a gift certificate for a massage. The recipient can then add items and personalize the kit for himself.

ABCDE Reframe: See Things from a Different Perspective

The ABCDE reframe technique, a key construct of cognitive behavioral therapy, builds on rational emotive behavior therapy, pioneered by psychologist Albert Ellis in the 1950s.[15] The basic idea is that adversity, or an activating event (represented by the letter A) doesn't directly cause the consequences we experience (represented by the letter C), though it usually feels as if it does.

The real culprit lies between A and C—the letter B,

for *beliefs*. It is our beliefs about the adversity or activating event that shape the consequences. Therefore,
changing our beliefs has the power to change the consequences.

The *D* in this model encourages you to dispute your
beliefs, or argue with yourself to change your point of
view. The *E* reminds you to energize new beliefs with
actions that will lead to favorable consequences. This
technique may sound relatively easy, but it can be very
hard to let go of your beliefs, even when you don't like
the consequences.

Cynthia's Story

Cynthia walked confidently out of her bedroom and
moved down the hallway ready for a day of greatness. She
had eased into her morning with a few minutes of meditation and yoga stretches, then selected a cream-colored
suit coupled with her favorite aqua-and-gold scarf to
highlight the green tones in her eyes. Even her independently minded African American hair was having a good
day. As one of the top real estate agents in Los Angeles, Cynthia felt calm and self-assured. It made her smile
to think about the people, couples, and families she'd
helped find happy homes.

As she reached the bottom of the staircase and turned

to enter the kitchen, Cynthia stopped as if she had been slapped across the face. Pots and pans filled the sink, and gooey spaghetti clung to the edges. Dirty plates, cutlery, and glasses sat abandoned on the counter, where red sauce congealed on every surface. She couldn't move. If she took one step closer, she was sure the bright crimson gunk would somehow leap onto her pretty suit and ruin it forever.

Cynthia's temper flared. The kitchen had been spotless when she'd gone to bed the previous night. Clearly her twenty-four-year-old daughter, Madison, a recent boomerang, had decided to whip up a late-night spaghetti dinner for herself and left this awful debris in her wake.

Cynthia felt hurt and angry. Her routine every morning was to pack healthful food to eat on the go; that's how she kept her forty-five-year-old figure lithe and trim. Now she couldn't get anywhere near her own refrigerator to take out what she needed. Didn't that ungrateful girl care about anyone but herself?

Yanking her cell phone out of her purse, the enraged mom punched out an angry text to the woman-child asleep upstairs: **u left dishes in the sink!!**

Cynthia paused before she hit the Send button. "Here I go again," she thought. Ever since Madison had moved back home to hunt for a job after law school, mother and daughter had been locked in a seemingly unending struggle. Cynthia no more wanted to play the angry mom-police than Madison wanted to be treated like a child. The previous two months had been absolutely awful for both of them.

You could view the emotional hijack Cynthia had experienced as she entered the kitchen as the main problem here. But after she took a deep breath and decided not to send the angry text, she faced a more serious, ongoing problem: Cynthia was wedged into a downward-spiraling, destructive rut with her daughter.

Cynthia used the ABCDE reframe technique to reframe the situation with Madison before her relationship with her daughter became irreversibly damaged. It was easy to see that A, the Activating event, was the hodge-podge of dirty dishes. She stopped, used what she had learned about reframing, and reminded herself, "B stands for what I Believe about this situation. I believe that Madison disrespects me and my house. She needs to be dragged out of bed to fix this, *or else*. I can't let her get away with this kind of behavior. It's my job as her mother to make sure she does the right thing or suffers the consequences." Cynthia felt good as she articulated her point of view. But how could she change things?

C, the Consequences of her belief, represented the present state of her relationship with Madison. As she surveyed the scene, Cynthia thought, "The tug-of-war between my daughter and me destroys my sanity, damages our bond, and certainly won't help me close my real estate deal today."

Cynthia knew that if she continued to D and Disputed her beliefs, she might improve their interactions. But that was the hardest part. Cynthia felt wronged by Madison. It didn't seem like a belief—more like a fact.

She struggled to think about the world from her daughter's point of view. Madison had worked hard to finish her bachelor's degree and graduated from law school with top grades. The glut of lawyers in a tough economy, however, had stymied Madison's best-laid plans. Most of her graduating class was still unemployed. The firm where she had been an intern the previous summer had informed her entire cohort that it was unable to offer any permanent jobs. Madison had put on a brave face and moved back home, and spent ten hours a day sending out résumés, networking, and doing everything she could to break the logjam. She'd landed only one interview so far.

Cynthia began to form another picture of the situation:

Okay, she's more self-centered at this point in her life than I would like her to be, but maybe that single-minded focus is what it will take to succeed as a lawyer. She's not lazy. She's not on drugs. She's not depressed. I guess I have to

realize that her actions are not aimed at me. If I take this personally, I react with too much negativity. I want us to act like two responsible people who share a house. I want her to take some ownership. And she can't do that if I constantly jump on her mistakes.

Cynthia moved on to step *E*—Energizing her actions around this new set of beliefs.

Instead of being a disciplinarian, I can focus on her admirable work ethic. I can back off and try to have a mature conversation with her about what I need every day... such as a clean, peaceful kitchen in the morning.

Cynthia summarized her thoughts in a brief written note to herself:

A—Activating event: grimy kitchen
B—Belief: disrespect
C—Consequences: unproductive, disintegrating relationship
D—Dispute beliefs: it's not personal
E—Energize with action: treat her as an adult, even if she doesn't act like one

Just as Cynthia was finishing the note to herself, Madison came down the stairs. "Morning, Mom!" she called. "Hey, I'm really sorry about the kitchen. I was in the library until it closed, and I came back late last night starved...and exhausted. I promise I'll get it cleaned up before I head out this morning."

Cynthia felt her energy, and her tension, lift as though gravity had ceased to exist.

In the business world, we most frequently see the need for an ABCDE reframe when thorny personality issues crop up. For example, Caroline, a French Canadian account executive for a telecom company, was tormented with negative feelings toward Bob, a senior executive she had to work with. She felt that Bob, who was based in Austin, Texas, was sexist, and lamented the fact that he had a great deal of influence over the decision regarding her next promotion. She also perceived him as disrespectful to her professional style and philosophy, despite the many successes she'd attained. She despised the man and could see no way to improve their working relationship.

I feel so stuck...and I hate this. He doesn't respect me, and it makes me so angry!

We walked Caroline through the ABCDE steps.

Clearly Bob was the source of some adversity (A) in her life. She believed (B) that his overall lack of respect for her achievements would have negative consequences (C)—limited career prospects.

Caroline's deeply held beliefs took some time to dispute (D). We focused on her belief that her relationship with Bob could not be improved. We suggested that she consider it not from a purely professional viewpoint but from a personal, informal standpoint. Although their professional styles clashed, Caroline knew that outside work, Bob was interested in the jazz music scene in Austin, and she admitted that it would be fun to find common ground with him there. To see Bob not as a monster but rather as a flawed human being like the rest of us helped Caroline put aside her rage and dispute her rigid opinions about him. Was it possible that he did want to support her, but that his macho style blocked their ability to connect?

To energize (E) her new belief, Caroline needed to take action. At their next encounter, she struck up a conversation about the Austin music scene and let him wax eloquent on his passion for the saxophone. Later she found a reason to take a business trip to Austin, where she arranged a dinner meeting with Bob and his wife at a live music venue.

Meeting his wife and discussing music instead of work helped me see a more complete picture of Bob as a husband, father, and jazz aficionado. I actually enjoyed spending time with him! It really surprised me. It will definitely improve our working relationship.

ABCDE Reframe: Tips

1. Go through the conscious relaxation reset before taking on the ABCDE reframe. You have strong feelings about the situation that activates you; you'll need to deescalate your emotions before you can reframe your attitude.

2. Most people struggle with the dispute (D) step. If you do, bring another person into the discussion who can help you find a new way to look at the facts. It may take several conversations with various people to truly shift your thoughts in a positive direction.

3. Be patient with yourself and the process. It takes time to recognize feelings, separate beliefs from reality, and truly comprehend the consequences.

4. The ABCDE reframe doesn't work unless you really want to change your outlook. You have to be so

sick of the situation and its impact on your life that you will let go of your beliefs—even when they are justified.

5. You can *help* others walk through the process, but you can't *inflict* it on them. As much as someone around you may need to reframe her attitude, she won't likely make progress until she virtually begs you for help.

Reversi Reframe: Turn Your Obstacles Upside Down

The Reversi reframe is a quick and easy way to flip your attitude from negative to positive. It's fun for teams, too.

When we use Reversi in a workshop, we hand out plain white index cards to the participants and ask them to write down a limitation or an obstacle on one side of the card. People have written things such as: "I'd like to earn an advanced degree, but I don't have the money or the time."

Next, we ask them to flip the card over and write the opposite statement on the other side...even if they don't believe it's true. For example: "I *do* have the money and the time to earn an advanced degree." Then we ask them to discuss both sides of their cards with others at the table, who may provide new attitudes, insights, and ideas. Often miracles occur.

Part of the magic of this technique is that you set up other people to feed you positive energy and ideas. If you approached a group of friends and told them, "I have no money or time to go back to school," they'd probably commiserate and tell you how severe their own limitations are. But if you come to them saying, "I want to have the money and time to earn a degree," they will more likely offer positive, creative input, such as online universities, or examples of friends who have accomplished this goal. Complain and the whole world complains with you; why not invite folks to brainstorm with you on positive outcomes instead?

Reversi can work when you do it alone as well. We once did this exercise on a radio show and afterward received a poignant e-mail from a listener:

> When you told us how to do Reversi, I wrote down that I would lose my house after my divorce was final. I flipped over the card and wrote: "I can keep my house after the divorce." It didn't seem even remotely possible at first, but as I read and reread the words, I suddenly realized that my mother was getting too old to continue living on her own. I knew she hated

the idea of a nursing home, and she was becoming increasingly frustrated with her situation. We agreed she would move in with me and use the money from selling her house to allow me to keep the home I love. Thank you, Reversi!

It seems so simple, but we've seen that just a little adjustment like this can trick our brains into seeing options that we were unable to conceive of before. Most often we experience limitations or obstacles as fact, so we don't bother to think creatively about them. Reversi gets you to try on the opposite perspective for a few moments without judging it. And in doing so, you give yourself the chance to succeed.

At one of our workshops, a division head at a Fortune 100 company wrote, "The executive committee didn't approve my budget increase, so I can't make the innovative changes in my department that I had planned."

He flipped the card over and wrote, "I *can* make innovative changes in my department without the budget increase." The exercise helped him see that he could review the old budget and cut some traditional, never-before-questioned line items, which would free up funds to support new, innovative initiatives in his division. Just that quickly, his thinking was unstuck!

One of the funniest Reversi situations we ever

encountered involved a recently divorced woman who asked for help figuring out what to write on the back of the card. On the front, she'd written, "SOBX."

Think about it. Titters spread around the room as people got the meaning of the acronym.

My ex-husband makes my life miserable. He doesn't pay child support on time, and he always disappoints the kids. How do I reverse that? Do I remarry him? Shun him?

We love to share this example of Reversi with a group and then ask the participants what they would have suggested to her. Some people say, "Love your X" or "Forgive your X." Almost no one ever reaches the conclusion that we suggested: she should write *her own name* on the back of the card. To label her ex-husband as the source of all her problems negated her own power. She has more control over her life than he does. Reversi almost always boils down to that same principle: the solution to your problems lies with you, not someone else.

Fritz, a senior executive at a major international chemicals company in the Midwest, encouraged his team to use Reversi for both personal and professional challenges. They found it to be so effective that they opted to make it a team-building exercise at their weekly meetings. At the start of each meeting, someone volunteers to share an obstacle or limitation—at home or at work—and then everyone takes five minutes to brainstorm ideas that can reverse it. The whole team empathizes with each person's challenges and pitches in to find solutions.

Reversi Reframe: Tips

1. Start with a limitation or an obstacle. Write it on the front of a three-by-five index card. Next, write the opposite—whether you believe it or not—on the back of the card. Let the statement you wrote opposing your limitations provoke you. What if this premise were true?

2. Enlist help. Our negative and limiting beliefs can be so deeply rooted that it sometimes takes another person to show us our options.

3. Make Reversi part of your routine. As the White Queen tells Alice, "I daresay you haven't had much practice. Why, sometimes I've believed as many as six impossible things before breakfast."

4. In the spirit of micro-resilience, do a Reversi quickly whenever you need it during the day. Bonnie, for example, may notice that she feels resistance before

giving a speech. An internal voice says things like, "I'm not ready. I don't want to go out there and face this difficult audience." Backstage she'll quickly say the opposite to herself, e.g., "I can't wait to be onstage!" It helps immediately. Flip the script in your head, and you push your emotions in a new direction.

PPP → CCC Reframe: Change Pessimism to Optimism

Even though we may think of ourselves—or like to think of ourselves—as optimists, sometimes small weeds of pessimism may be insinuating themselves undetected in our lives.

Take the following quiz to find out where you fall on the optimism–pessimism spectrum.

1. You have company over for dinner and the food is a disaster. You think:
A) I am a terrible cook
B) I picked the wrong recipe

2. You win an athletic contest. Your first thought is:
A) I am really good at this
B) I trained well

3. You do poorly on an important exam. Your internal response is:

A) I didn't prepare enough

B) I'm not as smart as others who took the test

4. A flattering mention of you appears in the company newsletter. You think:

A) Everybody gets this kind of recognition

B) I'm proud of what I accomplished

5. You have trouble finding a job. Your reaction is:

A) The economy is down all over the country

B) I'm not using my personal connections effectively

Martin Seligman observed that pessimists perceive the bad things that happen to them as *permanent, prevalent,* and *personal.* For example, if you answered that you are a bad cook, you're not smart, and "the economy is down all over" on questions 1, 3, and 5 respectively, you think that things are bad everywhere, that they won't change, and that you are in a particularly bad spot compared to everyone else. From that point of view, attempts to improve things are pointless. Seligman often refers to pessimism as "learned helplessness."

Optimists, by contrast, choose the answers "I picked the wrong recipe," "I didn't prepare enough," and "I'm not using my personal connections effectively." They see negative situations as changeable and don't take failure personally.

When good things happen, as in questions 2 and 4, optimists internalize them more than pessimists do: "I am good at this" and "I'm proud of what I accomplished." Pessimists distance themselves from their successes and treat good fortune as a temporary state of affairs.

Optimists say things such as, "This, too, shall pass" when bad things happen. Pessimists say it when *good* things occur.

If you find that you use *personal, prevalent,* and/or *permanent* language to describe a negative situation, ask yourself these questions to spiral upward:

- What is the *challenge* to be tackled?

- What *choices* can I make?

- What am I *committed* to?

This shift from PPP to CCC can help during an ABCDE reframe or Reversi reframe, too. When we focus on the *challenge* of an obstacle or the *choices* we have, we create a more positive energy than we do when we feel trapped, helpless, and angry. The question "What are you really *committed* to?" focuses on the desired outcome and the values involved. Often we must choose between feeling right and achieving the business or personal results we really want.

PPP → CCC Reframe: Tips

1. Keep a log of good and bad things that happen to you during the day. Jot down notes about how you explain these things to yourself and others. Do you deflect the good and internalize the bad, or vice versa?

2. Choose a buddy in your work or personal life and agree to look out for PPP language with one another. For otherwise optimistic people, PPP language can crop up in relation to a particular topic or situation. PPP perspectives can emerge at a certain time of day or when bad news is announced. We may be the last one to notice the times or places it shows up in our thinking. Having a buddy to notice can empower you to turn it around.

3. Make CCC a habit. Put it on your morning coffee mug or post the words where you will see them every morning: on your bathroom mirror, in your car, or on your computer. Every morning, remind yourself what you are committed to, what choices you have, and the challenges you are enjoying.

Daily Reframe: Improve Your Average

All the Reframe Your Attitude techniques we've discussed so far were designed as a response to negative situations. The Joy Kit provides emotional first aid, the ABCDE method encourages you to dispute your own negative beliefs, the Reversi reframe turns your obstacles upside down, and the PPP→CCC perspective helps turn pessimism into optimism. But even under the best of circumstances, you can be proactive in an effort to keep negativity at bay. Daily exercises in positive thinking can improve your outlook—i.e., create a "new normal"—in the same way that a gym workout builds physical muscle. Periods of conscious, intentional, positive focus each day significantly increase the efficiency of your neurological, circulatory, and immune systems. As you strengthen your positivity "muscles," you increase creativity, receptiveness to feedback, and teamwork skills.[16]

US senator Kirsten Gillibrand told us of a daily reframe she uses in her life, and it has become one of our favorites. We asked how she keeps herself resilient through all the challenges she deals with in Congress: constituent complaints, the frustrating, molasses-like pace of the legislative process, relentless media criticism, and political backbiting—not to mention the genuine problems of the people she represents, such as poverty, the aftermath of natural disasters, and lack of access to health care.

We do *gratitude*. My chief aide and I do it throughout the day and between every meeting if we can. We find a quiet place—on a plane, in the car, sometimes even in the ladies' room— and talk about something we're grateful for. It's amazing. If we didn't have this ritual, I couldn't get through the day.

No matter how daunting negativity seems to be, a subtle but deliberate shift in mind-set can make all the difference in our ability to cope with problems. Our friend Jay, a successful Hollywood screenwriter, memorizes his favorite inspirational quotations—from Mother Teresa to Matt Damon—and recites them every morning, whether he's driving, walking, or sitting in a Starbucks. Sometimes he says them silently to himself; sometimes he says them aloud. We once shared this ritual with him in Mexico as we watched the sun rise over a sacred mountaintop. This magical moment literally filled us with energy—and he does this every day! Senator Gillibrand salts positivity throughout her day rather than making it a specific morning or evening practice, but hers is still a proactive routine. Neither she nor Jay waits for something bad to happen. They flex their inner positive-strength muscles as a matter of course, even when things are going well.

Daily Reframe: Tips

1. Make a list of three things you are grateful for every morning before you get out of bed. Try not to repeat any items on the list for at least a month.

2. At the end of each day, write three e-mails to people who have done good things for you, telling them how much you appreciate their help.

3. Make a daily date with yourself to observe natural phenomena that you normally would take for granted—the sunrise, the sunset, the appearance of a star or planet in the nighttime sky, the crashing of waves along the shore. Treat these phenomena as gifts that you don't have to do anything to receive, and accept them with gratitude.

4. For a more intensive option, try a variation on the Buddhist loving-kindness meditation that Fredrickson used during her breakthrough research on positivity. This ritual can help you no matter what religion—if any—you follow. Sit in a comfortable, quiet place and take a few calm belly breaths (see page 78) to center yourself. Focus on your body and breathing. Send thoughts of peace and tranquility to yourself as though they were a gift—perhaps imagine yourself being filled with a warm golden light. Then

send those same loving thoughts outward, to others, in the following order:

- To someone you respect and revere—a role model, a teacher, a spiritual leader

- To someone you love—a best friend or family member

- To someone you feel neutral about—an acquaintance; someone you recognize but don't know well

- To someone you actively dislike—an enemy, an antagonist, a nemesis

Feel your connection to these people and send them positive messages, such as, "May you be well," "May you be happy," and "May you find peace." You will find that sending positive thoughts to others helps you accept yourself for who you are, no matter what mistakes you've made in the past.

REFRAME YOUR ATTITUDE: CONCLUSION

Certainly there are times when anger, sadness, and other negative feelings are entirely appropriate; permitting yourself and others around you to exhibit a full range of emotions supports your general wellness. Excessive, Pollyanna-ish idealism can lead us to ignore all sorts of important realities we must continue to manage, especially in the workplace. The key is to live at the intersection of realism and optimism, which, as much of the research we've presented shows, goes against our natural instincts.

To put this in perspective, think of A. A. Milne's beloved characters Tigger and Eeyore. These two polar opposites represent extremes of behavior and teach us about the perils of both blind optimism and relentless pessimism. But in the real world, we can use these cuddly characters to help us find a balance. Tigger gets into trouble by going off on his reckless escapades, and Eeyore depresses everyone in the Hundred Acre Wood with his habitually dismal pronouncements.

Our evolutionary wiring predisposes us to act like Eeyore a lot more easily and more often than we act like Tigger. Environmental influences work against us as well. Not only does our internal physiology pull us downward, we also get plenty of help from negative stories in the media, fearmongering politicians, and the emotional gravity of the Eeyores closest to us at work and at home. To achieve balance between our downward donkey and our upbeat orange tiger, we must fight against our nature *and* our nurture. Ask yourself, "Am I being a little too 'Eeyore' about this decision?" Or "Could I use a little more 'Tigger' in my attitude?" If the answer is yes, maybe it's time to make use of some of the tips in this chapter. You'll be surprised by the results you achieve. Choosing to be positive has a cumulative effect that can dramatically alter every aspect of your life.

The wonderful thing about Tiggers
Is Tiggers are wonderful things!

1. R. F. Baumeister et al., "Bad Is Stronger than Good," *Review of General Psychology* 5 (2001): 323–370.
2. P. C. Ellsworth and C. A. Smith, "Shades of Joy: Patterns of Appraisal Differentiating Pleasant Emotions," *Cognition and Emotion* 2 (1988): 301–331.
3. Martin E. P. Seligman, PhD, *Learned Optimism: How to Change Your Mind and Your Life* (New York: Vintage Books, 2006).
4. Michele Phillips, *Happiness Is a Habit: Simple Daily Rituals that Increase Energy, Improve Well-Being, and Add Joy to Every Day* (Springville, UT: Cedar Fort, Inc., 2013), 104.
5. B. L. Fredrickson and C. Branigan, "Positive Emotions Broaden the Scope of Attention and Thought-Action Repertoires," *Cognition and Emotion* 19, no. 3 (2005): 313–332; G. Rowe, J. B. Hirsch, and A. K. Anderson, "Positive Affect Increases the Breadth of Attentional Selection," *Proceedings of the National Academy of Sciences of the United States of America* 104, no. 1 (2007): 383–388; H. A. Wadlinger and D. M. Isaacowitz, "Posi-

tive Mood Broadens Visual Attention to Positive Stimuli," *Motivation and Emotion* 30, no. 1 (2006): 87–99; T. W. Schmitz, E. De Rosa, and A. K. Anderson, "Opposing Influences of Affective State Valence on Visual Cortical Encoding," *Journal of Neuroscience* 29, no. 22 (2009): 7199–7207; D. Soto et al., "Pleasant Music Overcomes the Loss of Awareness in Patients with Visual Neglect," *Proceedings of the National Academy of Sciences of the United States of America* 106, no. 14 (2009): 6011–6016, doi: 10.1073/pnas.0811681106.

6. C. E. Waugh, B. L. Fredrickson, and S. F. Taylor, "Adapting to Life's Slings and Arrows: Individual Differences in Resilience When Recovering from an Anticipated Threat," *Journal of Research in Personality* 42, no. 4 (2008): 1031–1046; J. R. Dunn and M. E. Schweitzer, "Feeling and Believing: The Influence of Emotion on Trust," *Journal of Personality and Social Psychology* 88, no. 5 (2005): 736–748; K. J. Johnson and B. L. Fredrickson, "We All Look the Same to Me: Positive Emotions Eliminate the Own-Race Bias in Face Recognition," *Psychological Science* 16, no. 11 (2005): 875–881.

7. G. Rowe, J. B. Hirsch, and A. K. Anderson, "Positive Affect Increases the Breadth of Attentional Selection," *Proceedings of the National Academy of Sciences of the United States of America* 104, no. 1 (2007): 383–388; A. M. Isen, K. A. Daubman, and G. P. Nowicki, "Positive Affect Facilitates Creative Problem Solving," *Journal of Personality and Social Psychology* 52, no. 6 (1987): 1122–1131.

8. B. E. Kahn and A. M. Isen, "The Influence of Positive Affect on Variety Seeking among Safe, Enjoyable Products," *Journal of Consumer Research* 20, no. 2 (1993): 257–270.

9. R. Raghunathan and Y. Trope, "Walking the Tightrope between Feeling Good and Being Accurate: Mood as a

Resource in Processing Persuasive Messages," *Journal of Personality and Social Psychology* 83, no. 3 (2002): 510–523.

10. C. Lee, S. J. Ashford, and L. F. Jamieson, "The Effects of Type A Behavior Dimensions and Optimism on Coping Strategy, Health, and Performance," *Journal of Organizational Behavior* 14 (1993): 143–157.

11. E. L. Garland et al., "Upward Spirals of Positive Emotions Counter Downward Spirals of Negativity: Insights from the Broaden-and-Build Theory and Affective Neuroscience on the Treatment of Emotion Dysfunctions and Deficits in Psychopathology," *Clinical Psychology Review* 30, no. 7 (2010): 849–864.

12. Ibid.

13. Kim Cameron, *Positive Leadership: Strategies for Extraordinary Performance* (San Francisco: Berrett-Koehler Publishers, 2008).

14. C. M. Youssef and F. Luthans, "Positive Organizational Behavior in the Workplace: The Impact of Hope, Optimism, and Resilience," *Journal of Management* 33, no. 5 (October 2007): 774–800; B. Medlin and K. W. Green Jr., "Enhancing Performance through Goal Setting, Engagement, and Optimism," *Industrial Management & Data Systems* 109, no. 7 (2009): 943–956.

15. A. Ellis, "Rational Psychotherapy and Individual Psychology," *Journal of Individual Psychology* 13 (1957): 38–44.

16. E. L. Garland et al., "Upward Spirals of Positive Emotions Counter Downward Spirals of Negativity: Insights from the Broaden-and-Build Theory and Affective Neuroscience on the Treatment of Emotion Dysfunctions and Deficits in Psychopathology," *Clinical Psychology Review* 30, no. 7 (2010): 849–864.

5

Refresh Your Body

Increase Your Fuel Efficiency

"To keep the body in good health is a duty, for otherwise we shall not be able to trim the lamp of wisdom, and keep our mind strong and clear."

—*Buddha*

STAN'S STORY

When you look up the phrase *man's man* in the diction-
ary, you might just see a picture of Stan. As a regional
executive for a manufacturing plant in Virginia, Stan is
almost *required* to go out with the boys every so often—
sometimes to play pool (and pick up the tab for the beers);
sometimes to do a little hunting during deer season.

From the very beginning, Stan embraced micro-
resilience with a passion. The science made sense to
him, and he wanted to do everything possible to make
life better for the union guys (and gals, too) who did the
hard work at his plant. The idea of manufacturing, for
most of us, conjures up images of grease-stained cover-
alls, noisy machinery, and grimy surfaces. But Stan's plas-
tics plant produces everything from medical injection
devices to cell-phone cases. The "floor" of his facility—
the enormous room where the products get built—looks
as pristine as a hospital operating room.

Before introducing micro-resilience to his team,
though, Stan tested it on himself. He would never waste
his employees' precious time with a newfangled idea if he
didn't have a good experience with it personally. And the

first Framework he dove into was Refresh Your Body—specifically, the part about hydration. As Stan puts it:

> For about two months now, I've put aside my usual soda and started hydrating only with water...except for my morning coffee, of course. The first thing I noticed was that I didn't need my afternoon pick-me-up anymore. When one o'clock comes, I used to always grab a Mountain Dew or some other kind of soda to give me a burst of energy, to get me through. I don't do that anymore. Staying hydrated all day is actually better than getting a caffeine or sugar jolt in the middle of the afternoon.
>
> I know the water makes a big difference, because on the weekend or a day off I'll get out of the routine. By the end of the day I feel lousy. I have to hydrate every day now—it's almost like being addicted to feeling good.
>
> My job comes with a lot of pressure. When there's any downtime in the plant, we hemorrhage money. We have union negotiations, employee accidents...and the clients all want their outputs yesterday with zero errors. It's my job to keep everyone jumping—from the loading-dock workers to the programmers and designers.

Staying hydrated helps me to be high energy and relaxed at the same time. I don't know how to explain it. My body—this is going to sound funny...but when I'm fully hydrated, my body feels soft. Not soft like jelly; just relaxed. I don't get a headache. I don't get tense shoulders. I don't get a stomachache. My energy level is high, and I'm thinking more clearly. I can keep going all day and move around the plant, but I don't feel the discomfort I felt in the past.

Stan's praise for hydration highlights its positive effects on our everyday lives. But there's a second, equally important way to refresh your body: maintaining an optimal level of blood sugar. Taken together, hydration and glucose balance help keep your metabolism on an even keel and lend support to your efforts in all the other micro-resilience Frameworks.

REFRESH YOUR BODY: THE SCIENCE OF HYDRATION

There is no easy answer to the question of how much water one should drink each day for general good health and *macro-resilience*. It depends on your weight, the amount of exercise you get, the climate in which you live, and many other factors. The old adage of eight eight-ounce glasses (about two liters) per day is a good rule of thumb, but some people may need more.

Our *micro-resilience* perspective on hydration differs from the traditional point of view by putting attention on *when* you drink water in addition to how much. When you're under stress or a tight deadline, that trusty water bottle is often relegated to the far side of the desk and ignored. But those are the times when you need that hydration the most.

Studies point to immediate performance benefits from drinking water. Researchers in the UK demonstrated that test subjects who drank a pint of water before they performed challenging mental tasks had reaction times that were 14 percent faster than those of subjects who had not hydrated.[1] The same scientists showed that schoolchildren who drink more water than their classmates have improved attention spans and are better able to remember things.

If we get busier than usual and let our water habits fall by the wayside for a few hours or a full day, science tells us that our ability to hit our targets will decline.

A National Institutes of Health review of the research on water, health, and hydration[2] identified several studies in which mild to moderate levels of dehydration impaired performance in a range of cognitive areas, including short-term memory, perceptual discrimination, arithmetic ability, and coordination of movement with visual tracking.[3]

These and other related studies explain why water makes such a tremendous difference in Stan's day. Better memory, more facility with numbers, greater visual acuity, and closer eye-hand coordination are important elements of his job, along with interpersonal skills, construction of complicated gadgetry, and organization—all with a keen eye for efficiency and profitability.

Did you ever have a moment when your thought process felt stuck? Or you knew there was a better way to do something and you just couldn't see it? A quick drink of water may make a difference.

Our youngest daughter, Ella, is a terrific actress and loves to perform onstage. Last summer she proudly announced she had been cast as Beatrice, the female lead in Shakespeare's *Much Ado About Nothing*. We were thrilled, of course, and couldn't wait to see her embody one of the Bard's most subtle and sophisticated female characters.

The only downside to all this came when Ella discovered that Beatrice has more than a hundred separate chunks of dialogue, including some rather long and intricate monologues—in sixteenth-century Elizabethan English. And this was a summer stock production where the players had only about two weeks to rehearse!

"My head feels fuzzy," our frustrated thespian told us one day after almost an hour of going over her lines. "I'll never be able to learn all this."

"Drink water," we urged her, and we quickly explained to her the research and rationale behind our suggestion.

Fortunately, Ella was still young enough to accept advice from her parents. She drank some water, went diligently back to work, and noticed the difference almost immediately.

"It's so much easier to remember the words!" she told us. "My brain feels better."

Ella not only mastered her complex and extensive lines, she also gave the performance of her life as the independent and strong-willed Beatrice. Now, whenever she has to memorize anything, study for a test, or perform any kind of complicated task, you'll always see Ella reach for a bottle of water.

Hydration Affects the Other Micro-Resilience Frameworks

A further implication of the hydration research cited above is that our Refocus Your Brain tips won't work very well when your gray cells are parched. Because the brain is made up of more than 70 percent water, and the rest of our body is closer to 60 or 65 percent,[4] you may not even feel thirsty before your brain begins to experience a hydration shortage. Some experts encourage us to drink water *before* feeling thirsty to maintain optimal "body hydration status."[5]

Hydration affects our moods as well. The most consistent effects of mild dehydration reported by participants in the studies reviewed by the NIH include fatigue, confusion, and anger. Something as simple as low hydration could subvert you when you use the reset techniques to de-escalate a hijack, for example, or the reframe techniques to become more positive. Perhaps that's what Stan meant by feeling "soft" yet more alert and clearheaded. Routine anger, confusion, and fatigue resulting from chronic lack of fluids might have "hardened" him in a way that drained his energy and impeded his performance.

Poor overall physical health makes a resilient life very difficult, too. The NIH review concludes that dehydration can have a negative effect on the kidneys, heart, digestion, and skin. Conversely, good hydration is associated with a reduction in chronic problems such as headaches, urinary tract infections, hypertension, and more. Stan discovered for himself that drinking water *consistently during the day* eliminates the pain and discomfort he'd grown accustomed to living with.

REFRESH YOUR BODY: HYDRATION SOLUTIONS

We've put thousands of people through our Micro-Resilience program, and most of them have been able to solve their hydration problems by taking a few easy steps to integrate water into their daily routines. Here are some tips to make hydration fun—and appealing.

Hydration: Tips

1. Get a new water bottle you really like. Pick an unusual color, put stickers on it, or go for a sleek design that pleases your sense of style. One woman used a Sharpie to write an inspirational phrase— "Happy Hydration"—on the side of her bottle.

2. Keep a bottle of water on your desk and another in your car. An insulated mug will help keep the water in your car from becoming too hot in the summer and from freezing in the winter.

3. Bonnie freezes chopped-up fruit, such as strawberries and oranges, and uses them as ice cubes. They taste great and remind her of the water served at fancy resorts and spas.

4. Herbal tea is essentially flavored water and provides almost the same hydration value. Allen makes mint herb tea and chills it in pitchers so that he has easy access to it throughout the day.

5. When you feel hungry, drink a glass of water first. Mild hunger and mild thirst can feel similar.

6. Ask for water in restaurants if they don't offer it right away.

7. Drink a glass of water before and after every meal—that will cover at least six glasses per day and help reduce your overall food intake if that is a challenge for you.

8. Our nutritionist advised us to match each ounce of the caffeinated and alcoholic beverages we drink with an ounce of water to offset their dehydrating effects.

9. Time your hydration so that you drink the majority of your water during the most difficult and challenging part of your day.

REFRESH YOUR BODY: THE SCIENCE OF GLUCOSE BALANCE

Glucose, or blood sugar, has an impact on hour-by-hour resilience that parallels that of hydration. Omnipresent grocery stores, refrigeration, and restaurants make food available to us at all times, but we can still get hungry: we could be stuck in an airplane being held on the tarmac, trapped in back-to-back meetings at work, or committed to being the chauffeur for the kids' after-school activities. Despite all our modern conveniences, it's entirely possible that we may be deprived of food for hours on end.

A metabolic "big spender," the human brain demands 20 to 25 percent of our daily calorie intake even though it comprises only 2 percent of our body weight.[6] In particular, the executive functions of the brain— decisions, persistence at mental or physical tasks, logical reasoning—consume far more glucose than cognitive events that happen automatically.[7] Because only small amounts of glucose are present in the brain at any one time, and they can be depleted within five to ten minutes if they're not replenished, executive brain function is highly vulnerable to the availability of glucose in the bloodstream.[8] If we neglect to eat often enough, we risk confusion, indecisiveness, and frustration.

When your blood sugar falls, your ability to exert self-control falls, too.[9] Ever heard the word *hangry*? The longer it is since we've eaten, the harder it is to control our emotions; we flip into rage or tears seemingly at the drop of a hat. Anxiety is also exacerbated by hypoglycemic episodes (periods of abnormally low blood glucose levels).[10] An advertising campaign once proclaimed, "You're not you when you're hungry." This is a fundamental truth we can all attest to.

Psychologist Matthew Gailliot speculates that the high-order, complex executive functions of the brain developed late in the evolutionary process and are thus the first to go when resources become scarce—a "last-in, first-out" system. Your advanced brain activities—such as emotional control—will be sacrificed long before your breathing, heart rate, and other vital functions are. The primitive self shoves aside our evolved self and takes over when glucose is low. Self-control—the ability to redirect our primitive impulses for food and sex, to overcome laziness, and to channel our anger into something more productive—requires incredible amounts of energy. Balanced and consistent glucose levels can support executive function and help keep our primitive selves in the background.

If we avoid even what passes for "normal" fluctuation in blood sugar, we may reap a massive payoff.[11] Self-control is perhaps the one executive function most sensitive to glucose variation, and evidence links good self-regulation to healthy interpersonal relationships, popularity, good mental health, effective coping skills, low levels of aggression, and high academic performance, as well as to a reduction in susceptibility to drug and alcohol abuse, criminal behavior, and eating disorders.[12]

Having extremely elevated levels of glucose (hyperglycemia) doesn't mean the brain works better, either. High blood sugar over time can damage cells throughout the body, including in the brain, in various ways. The trick is to like your glucose levels the way Goldilocks likes her porridge: not too hot, not too cold, but just right.[13]

REFRESH YOUR BODY: GLUCOSE-BALANCE SOLUTIONS

To balance your blood glucose levels, you have to find foods that work with your lifestyle and taste preferences. We can't tell you exactly what foods those will be, so you'll have to invest some time and energy to figure it out for yourself. A good place to start is by finding out the glycemic index (GI) of the foods you eat. The GI system was originally developed to help diabetics understand how much certain foods would increase their blood sugar level, but we can all use it to micromanage our glucose and smooth out the highs and lows.

When you eat foods with a high GI index, like cake and candy, your blood sugar level rises rapidly. Under normal (nondiabetic) circumstances, insulin kicks in to balance this spike, and your blood sugar level drops. You are probably familiar with the feeling: an intense sugar high followed by an energy crash that leaves you horizontal on the nearest sofa. Foods with a low glycemic index, on the other hand, don't spike your blood glucose. They give you a smoother energy ride that lasts longer. Foods such as oatmeal, eggs, nuts, and vegetables have a low glycemic index.[14]

You may be surprised, however, when you take a close look at the numbers. Raisins and dried figs have nearly double the GI of fresh fruit. It's a good idea to do your research by consulting reputable sources, such as the charts provided by the Mayo Clinic and the National Institutes of Health.

Low-Glycemic Snacks

- Eggs

- Hummus

- Meat

- Milk

- Soy milk

- Nuts

- Vegetables

- Yogurt

- Berries

- Peaches

- Plums

- Cheese

- Edamame

- Jerky

- Protein shakes (with low or no sugar)

You don't have to go to extremes and limit yourself to only low-glycemic foods, either. In small quantities, medium- and high-glycemic foods can be combined with low-glycemic foods to create a balanced meal or snack. We suggest you check with a professional—a doctor or a nutritionist—before you create your personal eating plan.

Glucose Balance: Tips

1. Eat at home as much as possible; feel at home when you can't. At home you can control how much sugar,

processed flour, and other high-glycemic ingredients end up in your meals. When dining out, remember that you can ask for something that isn't on the menu, such as a plate of grilled vegetables or a plain grilled chicken breast. You don't have to settle for the entrée on the menu that seems like the least of all evils. Ask for what you want. It may seem embarrassing at first, but you'll have the last laugh, because you'll be the healthiest and happiest person at the table.

2. Carry food with you. Whether you travel two or three weeks out of every month, as we do, or your traveling is limited to running errands around the neighborhood, carry food with you to help prevent you from making bad choices. The world is not a friendly place for low-glycemic foods. If you see apples on sale in the airport, they are usually displayed right next to the potato chips. Since your judgment and self-control fly away when your blood sugar falls, it's just not a fair fight. The healthiest people we know carry snacks that they enjoy so that they don't get waylaid by high-glycemic foods.

3. Eat lots of fruits and vegetables. You don't have to be a vegetarian, but make sure you get lots of nature's bounty. Most Americans don't. Prepare grapes, carrot sticks, or sliced cucumbers so you can take them to work or eat

them on the go. Put small leaves of romaine lettuce in a bag and eat them as you would potato chips.

4. Protein shakes help. We've experimented with a wide range of them to find something that tastes good without excessive amounts of sugar; HMR and Beachbody are two favorites.[15] [16] Do your own taste tests. It may not be possible to determine the exact GI of your shakes, but choosing lower-sugar, lower-carb options is common sense. We are not fans of most protein or granola bars because they usually have a lot of refined sugar, white flour, and other high-calorie ingredients. If they don't, they generally taste terrible. That's our opinion; you choose what works best for you.

5. Be aware of your feelings. Often we get so busy thinking, working, and doing that we don't realize what's going on in our bodies. Monitor yourself for thirst, hunger, and the early warning signs of hazardously low glucose levels, such as fuzzy thoughts and losing your temper.

6. Access information. Numerous websites and books provide suggestions for shopping, recipes, and snacks. There is even a book called *Glycemic Index Diet for Dummies*.[17]

7. Get the support you need. Sticking to a new food regimen isn't easy. It's helpful to work with a buddy, join a group, or track your food intake with an app. Bonnie uses an online Weight Watchers coach for ideas, encouragement, and long-term support. Allen relies on his Atkins diet iPhone app. You can also enlist the people you see every day—coworkers, clients, family, and friends—to help you meet your goals. When teams of people who work together go through our micro-resilience training as a group, they find it much easier to build good habits, such as continuous water consumption and a diet of low-GI foods, into their lives at the office. If Refresh Your Body becomes part of the group culture, it has a better chance of success.

REFRESH YOUR BODY: CONCLUSION

Imagine one morning you step into the garage and see your five-year-old Chevy replaced by a beautiful, sleek, red Ferrari convertible. You slide behind the steering wheel and immediately feel every part of your body snugly supported by the ergonomically designed seat. As you punch the starter button, twelve perfectly tuned Italian cylinders come to life with a throaty roar. No matter how twisty the terrain, you blast around the curves like a champion race-car driver, supremely confident in the unlimited capabilities of the exquisite machine around you. Every movement is smooth and effortless, yet filled with the thrill of power.

But what happens if you don't give your new ride the resources it needs to deliver the super-high performance it was designed for? Use the wrong kind of oil, and all those pistons will soon lose their ability to hum along in perfect synchrony. Put cheap, low-octane gas in the tank, and the fuel injectors won't function at full power. Keep up this abuse, and your masterpiece of engineering will become nothing more than a ridiculously expensive boat anchor.

The human capacity for complex thinking and subtle social interaction is as dependent on a consistent supply of high-performance fuel and fluids as a Ferrari. If you treat yourself like the finely tuned machine you are, you'll get more of the amazing performance you were designed to produce. You can metaphorically trade in your five-year-old sedan for that supercharged sports car whenever you're ready.

---

1. C. J. Edmonds, R. Crombie, and M. R. Gardner, "Subjective Thirst Moderates Changes in Speed of Responding Associated with Water Consumption," *Frontiers in Human Neuroscience* 7 (2013): 363.

2. B. M. Popkin, K. E. D'Anci, and I. H. Rosenberg, "Water, Hydration, and Health," *Nutrition Reviews* 68, no. 8 (2010): 439–458.

3. C. Cian et al., "Effects of Fluid Ingestion on Cognitive Function after Heat Stress or Exercise-Induced Dehydration," *International Journal of Psychophysiology* 42 (2001): 243–251; C. Cian et al., "Influence of Variations of Body Hydration on Cognitive Performance," *Journal of Psychophysiology* 14 (2000): 29–36; P. M. Gopinathan, G. Pichan, and V. M. Sharma, "Role of Dehydration in Heat Stress-Induced Variations in Mental Performance," *Archives of Environmental Health* 43 (1988): 15–17; K. E. D'Anci et al., "Voluntary Dehydration and Cognitive Performance in Trained College Athletes," *Perceptual and Motor Skills* 109 (2009): 251–269.

4. H. H. Mitchell et al., "The Chemical Composition of the Adult Human Body and Its Bearing on the Biochemistry of Growth," *Journal of Biological Chemistry* 158 (1945): 625–637.

5. E. Jéquier and F. Constant, "Water as an Essential Nutrient: The Physiological Basis of Hydration," *European Journal of Clinical Nutrition* 64 (2010): 115–123.

6. R. I. Dunbar, "The Social Brain Hypothesis and Its Implications for Social Evolution," *Annals of Human Biology* 36, no. 5 (2009): 562–572; John J. Ratey, MD, *A User's Guide to the Brain: Perception, Attention, and the Four Theaters of the Brain* (New York: Pantheon, 2001).

7. M. T. Gailliot, "Unlocking the Energy Dynamics of Executive Functioning: Linking Executive Functioning to Brain Glycogen," *Perspectives on Psychological Science* 3 (2008): 245.

8. John J. Ratey, MD, *A User's Guide to the Brain: Perception, Attention, and the Four Theaters of the Brain* (New York: Pantheon, 2001).

9. M. T. Gailliot et al., "Self-Control Relies on Glucose as a Limited Energy Source: Willpower Is More than a Metaphor,"

Journal of Personality and Social Psychology 92 (2007): 325–336.

10. Daniel G. Amen, MD, *Change Your Brain, Change Your Life: The Breakthrough Program for Conquering Anxiety, Depression, Obsessiveness, Lack of Focus, Anger, and Memory Problems.* (New York: Harmony, 2015).

11. M. T. Gailliot et al., "Self-Control Relies on Glucose as a Limited Energy Source: Willpower Is More than a Metaphor," *Journal of Personality and Social Psychology* 92 (2007): 325–336.

12. C. N. DeWall et al., "Violence Restrained: Effects of Self-Regulation and Its Depletion on Aggression," *Journal of Experimental Social Psychology* 43 (2007): 62–76; A. L. Duckworth and M. E. P. Seligman, "Self-Discipline Outdoes IQ in Predicting Academic Performance of Adolescents," *Psychological Science* 16 (2005): 939–944; E. J. Finkel and W. K. Campbell, "Self-Control and Accommodation in Close Relationships: An Interdependence Analysis," *Journal of Personality and Social Psychology* 81 (2001): 263–277; M. T. Gailliot, B. J. Schmeichel, and R. F. Baumeister, "Self-Regulatory Processes Defend against the Threat of Death: Effects of Self-Control Depletion and Trait Self-Control on Thoughts and Fears of Dying," *Journal of Personality and Social Psychology* 91 (2006): 49–62; Michael R. Gottfredson and Travis Hirschi, *A General Theory of Crime* (Stanford, CA: Stanford University Press, 1990); D. Kahan, J. Polivy, and C. P. Herman, "Conformity and Dietary Disinhibition: A Test of the Ego-Strength Model of Self-Regulation," *International Journal of Eating Disorders* 32 (2003): 165–171; T. C. Pratt and F. T. Cullen, "The Empirical Status of Gottfredson and Hirschi's General Theory of Crime: A Meta-Analysis," *Criminology* 38 (2000): 931–964; Y. Shoda, W. Mischel, and P. K. Peake, "Predicting Adolescent Cognitive and Self-Regulatory

Competencies from Preschool Delay of Gratification: Identifying Diagnostic Conditions," *Developmental Psychology* 26 (1990): 978–986; J. P. Tangney, R. F. Baumeister, and A. L. Boone, "High Self-Control Predicts Good Adjustment, Less Pathology, Better Grades, and Interpersonal Success," *Journal of Personality* 72 (2004): 271–322; K. D. Vohs and T. F. Heatherton, "Self-Regulatory Failure: A Resource-Depletion Approach," *Psychological Science* 11 (2000): 249–254.

13. Larry Husten, "Lancet: Researchers Find Goldilocks Effect in Glucose Control for Diabetes," *Cardio Brief* (blog), January 26, 2010, http://cardiobrief.org/2010/01/26/lancet-researchers -find-goldilocks-effect-in-glucose-control-for-diabetes/.

14. Meri Raffetto, *Glycemic Index Diet for Dummies* (Hoboken, NJ: For Dummies, 2010); Dr. Eric C. Westman, Dr. Stephen D. Phinney, and Dr. Jeff S. Volek, *The New Atkins for a New You* (New York: Touchstone, 2010).

15. www.hmrprogram.com.

16. www.beachbody.com.

17. Meri Raffetto, *Glycemic Index Diet for Dummies* (Hoboken, NJ: For Dummies, 2010).

6

Renew Your Spirit

Tap into the Power of Purpose

The two most important days in your life
are the day you are born...
and the day you find out why.

—*Mark Twain*

THE BRICKLAYERS' STORY

Walking down a road, a man encounters a bricklayer and asks, "What are you doing?"

"Laying bricks," the mason responds, shrugging his shoulders.

A little farther down the road the wanderer sees another bricklayer working on the same project and asks again, "What are you doing?"

"Building a wall," she replies, pointing her trowel toward the obvious evidence.

After continuing some distance along this wall, the itinerant traveler encounters a third layer of bricks. "What are you doing?" he asks again.

"Constructing a cathedral!" answers the worker, looking reverently at the empty space where the cathedral would one day rise up in magnificence.

Finally, upon approaching a fourth laborer, the man asks, "What are you doing?"

"Worshipping God," comes the quiet response as the worker lovingly smoothes mortar between two perfectly aligned bricks.

—*Anonymous*

EMILY'S STORY

Emily sat quietly in her favorite wicker chair and surveyed the details of her beautiful Victorian home along the shores of Lake St. Clair. Over the previous twenty-five years, she and her husband, Lee, had meticulously restored their beloved gingerbread house to its original late-nineteenth-century glory. The renovation was, in many ways, a testament to Emily herself and her ability to see past the layers of mediocrity that had shrouded this unpolished gem. But at a certain point, her glorious surroundings made her feel as if she were trapped in a ditch—a comfortable ditch, but a ditch nonetheless.

Emily was an avid photographer, had degrees in both business and law, and was the most sought-after business editor and writer in the area. She wrote fiction in her spare time, and she volunteered her writing services to her church and local charities. But while Emily thrived in many ways, her daily existence lacked something. She was productive but not prosperous; diligent but not delighted. It was difficult to pin down exactly what was amiss—it was like that nagging feeling you get when you know you've forgotten something but can't seem to remember what it is. Emily's days didn't have a certain...deliciousness, as if she were missing an ingredient in her favorite soup. It was still quite good, but she knew she wanted more. As she told us:

> I am excited about so many things in my life—growing my business, writing fiction, and traveling. But at the age of fifty-five, I don't have the same gusto as I did when I was younger. I'm not as eager to make changes or take on new challenges as I used to be. Even though my hair went prematurely gray several years ago, I'm not ready for my life to go prematurely gray, too! I'm just looking for more...oomph.

"You haven't mentioned your sense of purpose—are you clear about it?" we asked her during a coaching session. As we'd discovered over the many years we spent developing our Micro-Resilience program, a sense of purpose, for many people, is a close cousin to "oomph."

Emily's brow furrowed as she thought about this. "Do you mean my long-term goals? Is that what you mean by purpose?"

It was a good question. When asked about their purpose, most people think about the future. Purpose can seem synonymous with long-term goals because both act as compasses that guide you on life's paths and let you know when you take a wrong turn. But your purpose is much more than your goals. No matter how much you care about your goals, they can exhaust you. A teacher who aims to become a school principal might find himself burned out if the frustrating politics of parents, teachers, and government regulations overshadow the satisfaction he gets from changing children's lives. A stay-at-home mom who runs for the school board to improve the quality of education in her district may eventually become discouraged by the red tape she encounters.

Purpose, when it stays more salient than our goals, invigorates us. Did you ever get lost in a task you love so completely that when you lifted your head, hours had flown by? When you feel a powerful passion, you can stay energized on a task through long hours and overcome seemingly insurmountable obstacles.

Still, no matter how clear and noble our purpose is, we need to revitalize it from time to time. Once we talked this through with Emily, she realized that her sense of purpose was far murkier than she'd thought.

When you put it that way, if you asked me right now what my purpose is, I don't think I could tell you.

This isn't unusual. Most of us treat goals as a sufficient substitute for purpose, and we don't realize when our internal compass is in need of recalibration. A lack of purpose doesn't hit you like a ton of bricks; it slowly paints the world in a slightly different hue. Only when asked point-blank questions such as, "What is your purpose?" or "Are you good at your purpose?" do we stop for a moment and realize it might be time for a spiritual "upgrade."

RENEW YOUR SPIRIT: THE SCIENCE

Scholars in the fields of philosophy, religion, psychology, and business management, among others, have written about the phenomenal power of purpose. Many of the greatest ideas in these fields—such as Abraham Maslow's famous hierarchy of needs[1] and Søren Kierkegaard's existentialism[2]—have throughout history underscored humanity's need to live for something beyond mere survival and material goods.

World-renowned neurologist and Holocaust survivor Viktor Frankl found that a clear sense of purpose made the difference between life and death in the hopeless hellhole of a Nazi concentration camp during World War II. He told the story of a man who had a vivid dream that the war would end and he would be liberated from the camp on a particular day: March 30. For weeks the dream strengthened his friend with hope. His eyes seemed brighter; his step quicker. However, as the date grew nearer and it became clear that the war was not at an end, Viktor's friend grew ill and feverish. On March 31, he died of typhus. The loss of his sense of purpose devastated this desperate man's immune system—and he just stopped fighting.[3]

Amid the horror of Auschwitz and Dachau, Frankl witnessed many more examples of those who lost the will to live, gave up hope, and died. He attributed his own survival, in part, to his profound desire to find meaning in the ghastly suffering around him and write about it afterward. His conclusions, in essence, state that unlocking your purpose not only raises you above drudgery but also bolsters your courage—and even strengthens your life force—through the most harrowing situations imaginable.

In more recent times, studies such as the one led by Dr. Patricia Boyle at the Rush Alzheimer's Disease Center have underscored Frankl's observations by statistically linking a higher sense of purpose and directedness in life with lower mortality rates.[4] During the study's five-year follow-up period, those who derived meaning from life's experiences, who had a sense of intentionality and thus "high purpose," were about half as likely to die. Subsequently, a team of researchers led by Patrick Hill of Carleton University extended these findings beyond elderly populations across a much wider range of ages, including six thousand participants over a fourteen-year period.[5] "Our findings point to the fact that having a direction for life, and setting overarching goals for what you want to achieve can help you actually live longer, regardless of when you find your purpose," says Hill. "So the earlier someone comes to a direction for life, the earlier these protective effects may be able to occur."[6] This effect of purpose on longevity remained significant even when other indicators of well-being like positive emotions and positive relationships were taken into account.

In a completely different field, business experts describe how the individual power of purpose in leaders translates into stronger and more successful companies. Joseph McCann and John Selsky argue that purpose provides a strategic guidepost in the midst of turbulence, supports stability while business recovery coalesces, and facilitates agile decision making in times of transformation.[7] Peter Senge, author of the leadership classic *The Fifth Discipline*, says simply, "Real vision cannot be understood in isolation from the idea of purpose. By purpose, I mean an individual's sense of why he is alive."[8]

RENEW YOUR SPIRIT: SOLUTIONS

When we turn from scholarship to solutions, we find that Renew Your Spirit must be approached differently from the other Micro-Resilience Frameworks. We aren't able to immediately show most people how to use micro techniques to obtain hour-by-hour resilience, because most people don't have a clear sense of their overall purpose. As we saw with Emily, nearly everyone needs to step back and fine-tune their *macro* sense of purpose before we can help with the *micro* work. Renew Your Spirit is therefore the only Framework in which we recommend that you use both macro and micro techniques in order to reap the full benefits.

As authors, our overall conception of purpose is very much rooted in Viktor Frankl's idea that everyone is responsible for finding, defining, and claiming meaning—or purpose—in his or her own life; the answer is not given to you. In the foreword to Frankl's book *Man's Search for Meaning*, Rabbi Harold Kushner writes:

Terrible as it was, [Frankl's] experience in Auschwitz reinforced what was already one of his key ideas: Life is not primarily a quest for pleasure, as Freud believed, or a quest for power, as Alfred Adler taught, but a quest for meaning. The greatest task for any person is to find meaning in his or her life. Frankl saw three possible sources for meaning: in work (doing something significant), in love (caring for another person), and in courage during difficult times.[9]

Similarly, we treat purpose as something active and mutable, not static or predefined. To this end, we deconstruct purpose into two parts:

Purpose = Values + Goals

Why goals and values? The word *goals* implies action and direction, whereas the term *values* encompasses passion, belief, and joy. Goals without values are just actions without meaning. Conversely, values without goals are passive, not purposeful. Though there may be many other ways to define purpose, we've found this formula to be a handy way to break the concept down, distill it, then put it to work.

Values Detective Renew (Macro):
Examine Your Own Story

Exercises that give you a list of values and ask you to rank them are often confounding. How does it help to decide that honesty is more important than hard work or that vision trumps compassion? We've even seen versions of these tests that ask you to assign dollar values to a selection of one-word traits. Our Values Detective technique takes a different approach.

Consider the following story:

> In 1926 a young Englishwoman, Joanna Field, began to feel that she was not living a truly authentic life, that she did not know what made her truly happy. To remedy this, she kept a secret journal in order to discover what specifically triggered the feeling of delight in her daily life. The journal was published in 1934. It was written, she confided, in the spirit of a detective who searches through the minutiae of the mundane in hope of finding clues.
>
> She discovered that she delighted in red shoes, good food, sudden bursts of laughter, reading in French, answering letters, loitering

in a crowd at the fair, and a new idea when it is first grasped.[10]

Our advice is similar: expand the very definition of values. Include your most important beliefs as well as everything that makes you *joyful*—a glimpse of blue between skyscrapers in the city; the sound of a child singing; sand between your toes at the beach. These emotional touchstones provide important hints about who you are and what matters to you.

When you approach your values as a detective, you find clues to your priorities everywhere. Where does your discretionary income go? How do you spend your free time? Some people travel to new places to learn, find adventure, or expand their horizons, while others may travel to the same place year after year for extended family gatherings. One is not better or worse than another, but each reflects different values. The truth is found in how you *live*.

Values are often best captured in the stories of our experience. Allen's grandfather owned a flour mill in rural Pennsylvania during the first half of the twentieth century. Farmers drove their grain trucks extra miles across the rugged country roads, past several other mills, to get to the Haines Brothers Flour Mill because they knew they'd get an honest price for their harvest. Most of the business was done by barter in those days—grain for flour—and other millers would hide stones in the flour sacks to make them heavier and cheat the farmer, but not Ira Haines. When Allen ponders his definition of the word *integrity*, his grandfather's story serves as a guiding light. When he's confronted with a difficult situation, he asks himself, "What would Grandpa do?" Personal stories resonate deep in our souls.

When Emily, the writer from Michigan, tried our Values Detective Renew technique, she hit on the values embedded deeply in her DNA.

> **The same concepts popped up again and again. I started to see what was happening— I was reminded of my core, of what my truth is, of what will never change. I realized that I was faithful, punctual, and loyal. I have a deep desire for excellence, a love of family, and a passion for writing. I value my honesty and my health. And I am grateful, so grateful, for what my life is and can become. The exercise made me dig down below the surface and find the bedrock of what makes me...me.**

Different people, of course, will come up with completely different answers. The process itself is as critical as identifying the results. What is revealed to each person comes from his or her individual personality, experience, and culture. Every set of answers is beautiful, unique, and real.

Values Detective Renew: Tips

1. Answer each of the "Detective's List of Questions" that follows to explore the life experiences that underpin your personal values.

2. If your answers don't match what your values are, it may be time to rethink some of your lifestyle choices. We've had program participants who got a "wake-up call" from this exercise.

3. Try this exercise with a partner—maybe over coffee or a meal to savor the experience. One person can play the detective and interview the other person; then switch places. Remember that the person being interviewed is the one who writes down the answers. Family members, friends, and coworkers are all valuable collaborators. The process builds relationships and strengthens teams.

   - Whoever plays the detective embraces the role of investigator and tries to uncover deep truths behind the answers to the simple questions on the list. Feel free to add your own queries to the mix as you delve into the heart of the person you interview. Often the interviewee can't see her own unique values, the same way a fish may not be able to describe the water all around it. Be curious and tenacious; hold up a mirror.

- Make sure the interviewee doesn't just put down one-word answers but also reflects on what each answer reveals and writes those reflections down, too.

- When it's your turn to be interviewed, or if you're taking the quiz by yourself, remember that you don't have to produce an ordinary list—use the page as a space to express your feelings. Make some values bigger or brighter than others. Draw pictures if you like.

Values Detective Renew: Detective's List of Questions

- What kinds of things irritate you when others do them?

- How do you spend your free time? Examples include: going to parties, enjoying your social life, getting together with children and family members, volunteering, participating in faith-based activities, shopping, decorating, reading, walking, exploring nature, traveling, exercising, pursuing a hobby, furthering your education, relaxing, and watching TV. Pick your top two or three choices.

- How do you spend your discretionary income?

- Whom do you admire at work and elsewhere?

- What are the tasks you perform as part of your job that make the time fly by—the things you would probably do even if you weren't getting paid to do them?

- What are the tasks you perform that drain your energy at work and elsewhere?

- What brings you joy?

- What do people say you are good at? Do you agree?

- What do you find yourself teaching to others?

- When you choose someone to mentor, what characteristics do you look for?

- What are the most important things to teach a child—your own or someone else's?

- What are the most important qualities in a leader?

Life Goals Renew (Macro): Prioritize Your List

We find it frustrating and useless to rank order values. But goals, which are more concrete, can and should be prioritized. The late entrepreneur Scott Dinsmore, founder of a company called Live Your Legend, which helps people discover work they are passionate about, told a story about some advice that business magnate Warren Buffett gave his friend Steve. Buffett asked Steve to make a list of the top twenty-five things he wanted to do with his life in the following few years, then circle the five most important ones. The two men sat down and planned strategies for those top five priorities. Buffett then asked, "But what about the twenty things on your list that you didn't circle? What is your plan for completing those?"

Steve replied confidently, "Well, the top five are my primary focus, but the other twenty come in a close second. They are still important, so I'll work on those intermittently as I'm getting through my top five."

To Steve's surprise, Buffett responded sternly, "No. You've got it wrong, Steve. Everything you didn't circle just became your *avoid-at-all-costs list*. No matter what, these things get no attention from you until you've succeeded with your top five." The story may be nothing more than urban legend, but the point is a good one: *there is power in clarity and focus*. Prioritizing in this way doesn't usually turn your life upside down or challenge your belief systems; it just highlights what you most want to happen.

Emily made her list of life goals and systematically made choices among them. She ended up surprising herself with the three things that rose to the top: (1) helping others to pursue their passions with excellence, (2) spending a month every summer at the beach with her husband, and (3) mentoring young women. She summed up her experience this way:

> **Life Goals Renew had a profound effect on me. My original list started with many fun things to do and things that seemed so important at the time. What emerged at the end, however, was a clearer picture of what I am doing here in this world right now, what really matters. I could see that it might change over time, especially if life throws you a big curveball. Seems like a good idea to work through this maybe once a year or so.**

Life Goals Renew: Tips

1. Make a list of fifteen to twenty things you would like to have, do, or be in the life of your dreams—a life

that is rich in meaning and satisfying to you on every level. It's fun and exciting to boldly write down a description of your ideal life.

2. Circle the most important thing on the list, the one you would most like to have, do, or be if the others weren't possible.

3. Choose the second most important thing in the same way. If you could make only one more thing on the list a reality, which one would it be?

4. Continue on in this way until you have your top five. What bubbles to the top may pleasantly surprise you.

Tagline Renew (Macro): Articulate Your Purpose

According to Scott Snook and Nick Craig of the Harvard Business School, "Fewer than 20% of leaders have a strong sense of their own individual purpose. Even fewer can distill their purpose into a concrete statement."[11] It is commonplace for organizations, as a group, to take time to clarify their purpose into simple statements that can be kept front and center. These statements, or taglines, often change throughout the course of a company's—or brand's—lifetime. Think of Toyota: "Let's go places."

Think of McDonald's: "I'm lovin' it." Individuals, on the other hand, seldom tap into the power of branding for themselves.

It's true that people looking for a job, or people looking to fund a start-up business enterprise, create an "elevator pitch" that succinctly encapsulates what they have to offer. But this description should be ongoing, not just a one-time thing. Your personal tagline will evolve as you do, so it's important to keep examining it and updating it when necessary.

To harness the energy of your purpose, we suggest that you create a phrase that describes why you are here—your mission on earth. This simple tagline, a mini manifesto, will capture your unique style and contribution to the world so that others can easily recognize it. Why do people come to you for help? What do you do that is valued by others?

Snook and Craig wrote about a beverage company CEO who came up with this purpose statement: "To be the Wuxia master who saves the kingdom."[12] This reflects not only the CEO's love of kung fu movies, but also the inspiration he takes from the wisdom and discipline of ancient Chinese warriors. When he reflected on his professional experiences, this leader realized he felt most proud and alive when he took action and led his teams to success in high-risk, difficult situations. Scott Snook helped his wife, Kathi, create this statement for herself: "To be the gentle, behind-the-scenes, kick-in-the-ass reason for success." Kathi's proclamation drew on her experiences as both an army colonel and a stay-at-home mom; it also led her to run for (and win) a hotly contested committee seat on her local school board.[13]

Here are a few more examples of personal statements from leaders we have worked with:

- "To be the chief gardener"

- "To entertain, inspire, and elevate the vision"

- "To be the truth teller and cut through the crap"

- "To run toward the burning building and make everything better"

Even without knowing each individual's life story, you can see that you'd want all of these folks by your side in very different situations. You recognize these people as unique individuals. You understand their capabilities and what is important to them. In the same way, your own statement should validate how you "bring it" and why you are here.

After composing and disposing of reams of pages about her ideas and memories, Emily boiled it down to this concise, pithy phrase: "My purpose is to identify what is good and magnify it." Simple and elegant. This statement became Emily's foundation, both a tribute to her values and a distillation of her goals. Emily had found her purpose.

Tagline Renew: Tips

1. Take inventory of the things you have done well, enjoyed doing, and have been asked by others to do more of in the past. These experiences could arise from the jobs you've held, your volunteer activities, and even the role you play among family and friends.

2. Ask yourself the following three questions:[14]

   - What did you especially love to do when you were a child, before the world told you what you should and shouldn't like?

   - Write about two of your most challenging life experiences. How have they shaped you?

   - What do you enjoy in life that helps you sing your song?

3. Draft a purpose statement based on your personal inventory and your answers to the three questions

above. Your first attempt may come out full of jargon, platitudes, and convolution. Don't worry: this is just the clay you shape into something more useful and beautiful. Reduce the complexity and use simple words as you do so.

4. Choose words that have meaning for you, not necessarily for the people who will hear them. Personalize the language in ways that add inspiration, humor, and personality.

5. Check in with others who know you well in various contexts. Your statement should be something that people recognize as you.

6. Don't be afraid to change your tagline if it doesn't feel right. As you grow, you will want to reevaluate it from time to time. And you may just want to change it whenever you feel the need to be reinvigorated.

Touchstone Renew (Micro): Keep Purpose in View Every Day

Although Emily had gone through the process of examining her values, making a list of life goals, and writing a tagline, our work with her was not yet finished. While her macro work was commendable, in order to get the most out of this process, fully renew her spirit, and anchor herself on a day-to-day basis, she needed to use micro renewal techniques to apply this clarity of purpose to her daily life. We suggested that she start by creating a touchstone—a concrete, visual embodiment of her statement of purpose. She enthusiastically embraced this challenge. First she created a logo. She bought an old-fashioned, Sherlock Holmes–type magnifying glass and traced the lens onto a piece of paper. In the center she wrote the words "Identify the good and magnify it" in lovely, old-style calligraphy. She cut out the circle and taped it directly onto the lens of the magnifying glass, literally enlarging the words. She keeps this new touchstone by her bedside to ground her at the beginning and end of every day. She even took a picture of it and made it the screen saver on her computer and iPhone, so her purpose stays front and center for her at all times.

These may seem like simple things—a screen saver and an object by the bedside. But every time Emily catches a glimpse of the glass, she feels invigorated. When she's stressed, it reminds her to stay centered and focus on the positive. When she's worried, and the amount of goodness in the world seems infinitesimal, she knows she can use her gifts to help others.

Emily's parents were, at this point in her life, a huge source of her angst. Her father had early-stage dementia, and her mother was recovering from a broken hip. Preoccupied by endless doctor's appointments and hospital visits and the myriad details of elder care, Emily felt saddened as she watched her mom and dad suffer the effects of advancing age. To lift their spirits, she volunteered to write their annual Christmas letter, something that had always been an important part of their family's holiday celebration. But as she sat down at her computer, Emily wondered, *How am I to express the joy of the holidays when my family is in such distress?*

Emily reflected on her purpose and realized that she could be a magnifying glass for her parents and the rest of her family. As she looked at the words through the lens, Emily understood that she had the capability—and the responsibility—to unearth the delight buried beneath the suffering in her parents' lives. Energized, she wrote about the special moments she and her parents had experienced—the blessings and the triumphs that had brought them closer as a family. Instead of glossing over the tough times, she acknowledged them and expressed her gratitude.

I found pieces of joy inside myself that I could send to the people on our list to ignite their good feelings despite the bad things they might be facing, too.

Allen's Touchstone Renew

Allen often recalls his favorite touchstone renew exercise. He has been the CEO of several medium-size, high-growth companies that specialize in entertainment marketing. These companies produce theatrical trailers, TV commercials, posters, billboards, and all sorts of materials for every major movie studio and television network. You've seen his promotions for *Star Wars Episode I*, *The Lion King*, *Everybody Loves Raymond*, *CSI*, and many other popular productions.

Hollywood, Allen discovered, is a place where the vast majority of the people you meet are somehow involved in show business, either directly or indirectly. "Hollywood buzz" permeates the entire atmosphere of the west side of Los Angeles County. Allen would sit in a restaurant and hear the people at the next table banter about last weekend's movie grosses. On a shopping trip to buy sneakers for his daughter, he'd run into a studio head who wanted an update on the progress of the trailer for his or her latest blockbuster. He went to PTA meetings and sat next to Gene Simmons, Hugh Hefner, and Jodie Foster! It seemed as though there was no escape. Allen's suffocation by the glitz and glitter began subtly, beneath the surface, but it steadily grew stronger. His life became all about the game rather than the creative work—and gamesmanship was not why he'd come to sunny southern California.

Allen's purpose is to entertain through telling powerful stories. Whether he acts onstage, directs a film, writes a book, or transforms a two-hour movie into a compelling two-minute trailer, Allen is happiest when he makes a point or spins a yarn in a pleasurable and amusing fashion. To nurture his purpose, Allen remembered the spark that had initially drawn him to his passion: Disneyland.

When he was ten years old, Allen's parents took the family on a vacation that started in San Diego and continued all the way up the Pacific coast to Seattle, with stops along the way to see the sights. The sight Allen most wanted to see was Disneyland, the magical kingdom he drooled over on Sunday nights when he watched *Walt Disney's Wonderful World of Color* on TV. When the day finally came to set foot on that hallowed ground, Allen was more excited than he'd ever been before. He clearly remembers the moment he looked up at the arch just inside the main gate, saw a plaque (that still graces the entryway today), and read the words that would change his life: HERE YOU LEAVE TODAY AND ENTER THE WORLD OF YESTERDAY, TOMORROW AND FANTASY. He knew right then and there: taking people on that kind of journey was his purpose.

So when the atmosphere in Hollywood became so murky he couldn't see through it, Allen decided that the best way to get his purpose back on track was to return to his touchstone. Fortunately, Disneyland is just a short day trip from Los Angeles. He went to the park, passed under that inspirational archway, and found his favorite spot: a small wrought-iron bench directly across from the Mark Twain Riverboat dock, where Adventureland, Frontierland, and New Orleans Square converge in a festival of light and color. He sat there and just watched the people. Families holding hands, kids with ice cream, couples smooching—all walks of life; all races, nationalities, and cultures—having the time of their lives. "These are the folks we entertain," he thought. Allen made that pilgrimage many times, and every time he did, he felt his purpose reservoir fill to the brim.

Sylvia's Touchstone Renew

Another powerful example comes from Sylvia Mathews Burwell, the United States secretary of health and human services. Bonnie first met Sylvia when they were Rhodes Scholars together at Oxford. In addition to her exemplary career in government service, Sylvia has held senior leadership positions at prestigious humanitarian organizations. As president and founder of the Global

Development Program at the Bill & Melinda Gates Foundation, she led a team dedicated to the elimination of poverty throughout the world.

Most people probably think that the team of scientists, philanthropists, and other experts at the Gates Foundation merely sifts through mountains of proposals and send big checks to the most deserving charities and projects—as if they run a global beauty contest for great ideas. The reality, however, is far more complex, and far more impressive. The Gates Foundation doesn't just wait for requests to arrive in the mail. It initiates its own programs, some of which require cooperation from multiple foreign governments, large academic research institutions, and powerful private-sector firms. Sylvia and her team could at times get caught up in the complexity of facilitating cooperation among these powerful players and easily lose focus on the *why*.

Sylvia thought of a simple way to pull herself and her team back to their core sense of purpose. In the conference room where they met to hammer out strategy, she hung a large framed picture of a young African girl, emaciated from malnutrition yet wearing a warm, engaging smile that drew the essence of her soul right into your heart. Sylvia introduced the girl to her squad of professionals as their new "boss." After that, whenever they were in the midst of heated discussions, Sylvia or another member of the team would stop and ask, "What would the boss think?" To look into those big, dark eyes and see the vulnerable child whose future depended on their decisions often changed the dynamic of the conversation and forced the team to push back harder against so-called political realities. That simple touchstone inspired them daily to remember why they had taken their jobs in the first place.

Touchstone Renew: Tips

1. Brainstorm—by yourself or with your team—tangible and visible representations of the abstract feelings and ideas that fuel your purpose.

2. Choose a specific symbol or object that can instantly move, touch, and inspire you, as the families at Disneyland did for Allen. This will become your touchstone.

3. Put an image of the touchstone on your bathroom mirror, on the dashboard of your car, on your water bottle, or on something else you look at every day.

4. Use your touchstone as the wallpaper or screen saver on your computer or phone.

5. Carve out time to reflect on your touchstone each day: it could be in the gym, on your commute, or even at the dentist's office while you wait. These mini renewals are amazingly gratifying and invigorating.

Schedule Renew (Micro): Tailor Your Calendar to Your Sense of Purpose

Peter is one of the most driven people we've ever met. Near the top of his class at the Harvard Business School, he had a plum consulting job lined up before he graduated. He married Aisha, another staggeringly bright intellectual, with whom he set up housekeeping amid the stacks of books, papers, and other publications that feed their inquisitive minds.

Although he has the stamina of a thousand-horsepower diesel engine, Peter came to us one day with a challenge. He struggled to balance his supercharged ambition with his desire to be a supportive, loving husband to Aisha. He had already gone through many parts of our Micro-Resilience program, so he had made checklists and prioritized his various academic responsibilities. But finding a way to create emotional availability in his marriage had him stumped. Peter always gave 110 percent in everything he did, and he was concerned that there were never going to be enough hours in a day for him to accomplish everything on his plate and still have time for Aisha.

Together with Peter, we analyzed the various elements that make up his daily routine through a new, more "purposeful" lens, and fascinating revelations surfaced. As he described it:

> Let's say I have a paper to write. It's not a priority because I have top grades in all my courses and I'm taking the course pass/fail anyway. I could do good work and finish the paper in two hours, or I could do a really great job that would probably take me six hours. That's a situation in which my gut instinct says, "Oh, I want to do an incredible job and really knock this thing out of the park." But now I'm thinking: "That's four hours I could spend doing something much more important—whether something else for school or something personal." So I'll just do as well as I can in two hours, then submit it.
>
> Initially I felt a little guilty. But I reminded myself that I was doing this for a reason, a good reason: so I can spend more time with my

family. If you focus on that fact, the shift makes you happier. At first there was a feeling of loss. But then I had to flip my thinking to focus on what I was gaining.

Few people spend the *majority* of their time on the most purpose-centered things in life. But if you can shift a few minutes per day or a few hours per week from one column to the other—uninspiring to inspiring—you will add tremendous energy to your life. To examine the specific tasks on our schedules and make honest decisions about their relative importance to our purpose can open up a surprising amount of physical and psychological space. In the study of economics, scholars call that a *cost-benefit analysis*, but they seldom use purpose as a measuring rod. What are the costs of a particular activity versus the sense of purpose we derive from it? Once we reprioritize with a more profound outlook, we can see opportunities to rejuvenate, rather than debilitate, our lives.

Schedule Renew: Tips

1. Look at your schedule for today or for the next several days. Which activities are most aligned with

your purpose? Which things feed your spirit? Which things don't?

2. Eliminate one schedule item that does not align with your purpose. Even if it gains you only an hour or two for the week, it is a good start.

3. The following week, eliminate another activity on your schedule that does not feed your spirit. Can you delegate the task to someone else? We meet many people who hold on to chores they loathe at work when those same assignments could be done by others—many of whom are eager to take on projects that could help them grow.

4. If there is little or nothing on your calendar that fuels your purpose and passion, what can you *add* to your schedule that does? Block off time every day to take action that renews your spirit.

Flow Renew (Micro): Diagram Your Energy Levels

Bill Burnett, one of the professors at Stanford's well-known "d.school" (the Hasso Plattner Institute of Design), teaches a technique that resembles our schedule renew and helps people infuse their daily lives with meaning and purpose. Whereas the schedule renew technique helps you allocate more time to purpose-imbued tasks (and less to others), the flow renew technique helps you redesign the tasks you can't shorten or eliminate.

It's based on the concept of flow, pioneered by Mihaly Csikszentmihalyi,[15] one of the early proponents of positive psychology. Csikszentmihalyi noticed that there are moments when people achieve a complete oneness with their work, and at these moments, time seems to fly by, they forget to eat, and they lose themselves entirely in a task. He labeled this a state of flow. Though he and others studied this state from the perspective of psychology, flow has been observed and discussed for centuries in other fields of endeavor. It goes by various names, too, ranging from *wei wu wei* (doing without doing, a precept of Taoism) to *being in the zone* (in the vernacular of sports).

Burnett suggests that you keep a log of your energy levels while performing specific tasks during the course of a single week. Focus on the things you do repeatedly. You could even assign numerical values to your energy levels, perhaps on a scale from minus 10 to plus 10. Make note of the times you find yourself in a state of flow. At the end of the week, create a graph that diagrams your energy levels so you can see what moves you most. Your energy levels will be mapped along the vertical axis, and the tasks stretched along the horizontal axis. Starting in the middle of the energy axis, draw a straight line from left to right: this represents the midpoint of your energy; a neutral state in which you are neither depleted nor pumped up. Use the graph that Bill drew for himself as a model:

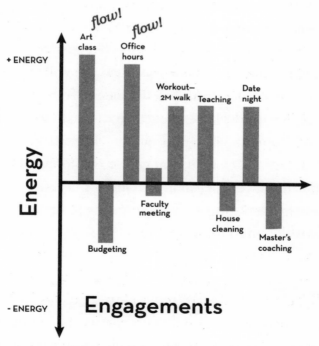

Chart reprinted with permission from
William Burnett and Dave Evans.

Then draw a thick vertical bar corresponding to each activity above or below the middle line, to represent your energy after each task. Did you feel drained? If so, then the bar drops below the middle line. Invigorated? Then the bar rises above the middle line. The height or depth of each bar shows the effect of each task relative to the others. The graph doesn't have to be scientific; make it a pictorial representation of your feelings.

What surprised Burnett most about his own graph was how much his Master's Coaching Class drained his energy, even though it should be a purpose-filled and rewarding activity. Upon reflection he realized that the environment for the class was full of distractions that made it difficult to focus. To make things worse, the students seemed to use the time to report everything that was going wrong. Burnett decided to restructure the class to change the environment as well as the negative discussion dynamic. Burnett converted an energy-depleting meeting into a more life-enhancing weekly commitment.

Flow Renew: Tips

1. Keep your flow log during the week. Map out the major activities in your life according to whether they add to or diminish your energy.

2. Where you see that your energy always drops, ask yourself if you can redesign the activity to have more flow. We have a friend who turned her monthly bill-paying chore into an "expense party" with her husband. They make martinis, download a new album, and prepare special hors d'oeuvres. What used to be another unpleasant task is now infused with things she values: good music, special food, and a sense of bonding with her husband. Can you rehab tasks that feel like drudgery to align them more closely with your values?

RENEW YOUR SPIRIT: CONCLUSION

Remember the opening lines of the old *Adventures of Superman* TV show? "Faster than a speeding bullet! More powerful than a locomotive! Able to leap tall buildings in a single bound!" Well, within every one of us lies a potential Superman with a potentially invincible strength: the power of purpose. We should all be humbled by what is possible when we exercise this power. Purpose can increase the profits of a company, as it did for Ben & Jerry's, or mobilize significant social change, as it did for groups such as Mothers Against Drunk Driving. Purpose has a mysterious quality that expands our life force beyond its normal capacities. The exact mechanism of this transformation may not be fully explained by science, but its power certainly can be harnessed.

While we have focused primarily on research in this book, we would like to note here that our faith in God plays a central role in our personal sense of purpose. Our religion provides us with direction, strength, and values, but the macro and micro work outlined in this chapter takes our purpose to a deeper level. Whatever your particular belief system may be, you may want to add this element to your purpose exploration as a way of further connecting to your inner feelings and motivations.

For Emily, this process served as a reminder that she was capable, competent, and a beacon of light to others. When she renewed her spirit and found her purpose, Emily's new direction had a ripple effect that people around her began to notice. One of her close friends was a PhD student who was disillusioned by his difficult academic experience. After spending some time with Emily, he said: "I see the stuff that is happening in your life, and it encourages me. I'm going to do what you are doing."

Emily soon entered a writing contest, something she would have never done before, and became a finalist. Her work caught the attention of a friend in the PR business who wanted to connect her with publishers. She entered another contest and won a photo shoot with a photographer who produced a new head shot that captured her energy and jubilance—not just her business acumen. She pitched her novel at a writers' conference and was excited about the possibilities.

If I don't secure a publication deal at the conference, I've decided I will self-publish the book anyway. One way or the other, I know my first book will come out this year. After years of keeping my finished novels on the shelf, I'm not waiting for anyone to give me permission!

We may not be physically able to leap tall buildings in a single bound, but sometimes it really feels as if we can.

---

1. A. H. Maslow, "A Theory of Human Motivation," *Psychological Review* 50 (1943): 370–396.
2. Søren Kierkegaard, *The Essential Kierkegaard*, ed. Howard V. Hong and Edna H. Hong (Princeton, NJ: Princeton University Press, 2000).
3. Victor E. Frankl, *Man's Search for Meaning* (Boston: Beacon Press, 2006).
4. P. A. Boyle et al., "Effect of Purpose in Life on the Relation between Alzheimer Disease Pathologic Changes on Cognitive Function in Advanced Age," *Archives of General Psychiatry* 69, no. 5 (April 2012): 499–505.

5. P. L. Hill and N. A. Turiano, "Purpose in Life as a Predictor of Mortality across Adulthood," *Psychological Science* 25, no. 7 (July 2014): 1482–1486.

6. "Having a Sense of Purpose May Add Years to Your Life," Association for Psychological Science, published May 12, 2014, http://www.psychologicalscience.org/index.php/news/releases/having-a-sense-of-purpose-in-life-may-add-years-to-your-life.html.

7. Joseph McCann and John W. Selsky, *Mastering Turbulence: The Essential Capabilities of Agile and Resilient Individuals, Teams and Organizations* (Hoboken, NJ: Jossey-Bass, 2012).

8. Peter M. Senge, *The Fifth Discipline: The Art and Practice of the Learning Organization* (New York: Doubleday/Currency, 1990).

9. Victor E. Frankl, *Man's Search for Meaning* (Boston: Beacon Press, 2006).

10. Sarah Ban Breathnach, *Simple Abundance: A Daybook of Comfort and Joy* (New York: Grand Central Publishing, 1994).

11. Nick Craig and Scott Snook, "From Purpose to Impact: Figure Out Your Passion and Put It to Work," *Havard Business Review* (May 2014).

12. Ibid.

13. Ibid.

14. Ibid.

15. Mihaly Csikszentmihalyi, *Flow: The Psychology of Optimal Experience* (New York: Harper Perennial Modern Classics, 2008).

7

Putting It All Together

You are the sum total of everything you've ever seen, heard, eaten, smelled, been told, forgot—it's all there.

—Maya Angelou

JOSH'S STORY

Those of us outside the medical profession tend to revere doctors. We endure embarrassment and inconvenience to obtain their advice. We sit in a waiting room littered with outdated issues of *Time* magazine as the clock ticks past our appointed time. Once ushered into an examining room, we obediently strip off our clothes, hop up onto an inconveniently high examination table covered with butcher paper, and dangle our feet over the edge like a kindergartener on a big kid's chair. When the doctor finally arrives, we stand up, sit down, roll over, and otherwise perform exactly as we're instructed without question or complaint.

We obey doctors because they have the power to repair broken bodies, prevent future calamities, and save our lives. We often put them on a pedestal and think that the mundane challenges of mere mortals are none of their concern. Right?

Not so much.

The life of a doctor today is filled with an array of financial and regulatory pressures and administrative chores, not to mention the anxiety of knowing that your work is sometimes a matter of life and death—and these responsibilities can become debilitating. Just ask Josh, a thirty-seven-year-old general practitioner.

My life felt like it was on the proverbial treadmill. I saw twenty to thirty patients a day—one after another—with very little time in between. I often worked through lunch. I gorged on fast food on the way home. I crashed into a coma at night. I woke up the next day and went to work, still tired. Weekends were for catching up on all the work I didn't have time to do during the week. That was it.

I was at a breaking point. I was so exhausted and overwhelmed that I began to dread every patient. Someone would check in, and I'd hear the person had an injury. Automatically I would think, *Oh my God, he's going to need stitches. I don't have the time. There are four other people waiting.*

I hate it when policy and procedure trump common sense, especially in medicine. All the pressure to push patients through faster made it impossible for me to give them even a small amount of attention and human compassion. And forget about filling out charts. By the weekend I could have a hundred charts on my computer waiting for me. People say, "TGIF— woo-hoo! Here comes the weekend." For me, the weekend was awful.

Occasionally slipping into a last-minute seat at a larger-than-life Broadway musical gave me an escape from my bleak day-to-day reality. This one guilty pleasure kept me going.

Josh felt trapped. He was consumed by his work, didn't have many friends, and couldn't see any way out. Although it was frustrating, he didn't want to give up his career, which still gratified him in many ways. He couldn't imagine any other life for himself. The unknown is uncomfortable—so much so that we often can't conceive of anything beyond what we see. He felt as though he had no choices whatsoever.

But the more he heard about the techniques of micro-resilience, the more hopeful Josh became. The idea of zone refocus made him realize he didn't have to read his e-mail as soon as every message came in during the day. He could make his time with patients one big zone in which he could focus exclusively on them:

Most of my job isn't e-mail-based. But after a big national company bought our practice,

we started getting all these inane corporate announcements along with reprimands for not following all their corporate guidelines, policies, and procedures. It seemed like they created a new rule almost every day. The e-mails were driving me crazy. But I realized none of these things were urgent, so I stopped reading them when I have more important things to do. On my busiest days, I don't read e-mail at all. I have so much less stress!

To address the adrenaline rush of concerns he felt every time he heard a new patient check in, Josh began using the labeling reset and a quick Reversi reframe. When worst-case scenarios played through his head, he reminded himself that he was awfulizing and flipped the script to a more positive, medically constructive focus.

It doesn't come naturally; my gut reaction when I see another patient checking in is very negative. I have to make an effort to turn myself around. When I feel myself getting worked up, I use labeling and Reversi...and they work! I catch myself saying, "You know what? This is going to be another interesting person I can help."

Next, Josh dealt with the exhaustion he was feeling as a result of his long hours of nonstop work. Rather than working through lunch, he began to take breaks every two and a half hours.

I set alarms on my phone throughout the day— silent alarms so they won't startle a patient. When I see it's gone off, I finish with my patient and then take a fifteen-minute break to drink water, eat the nutritious food I brought in, and listen to my special playlist of uplifting, energizing music. It's really making a difference. At the end of the day I can do things with new friends or even use that gym membership I was wasting money on before.

Micromanaging his metabolism during the day (the glucose-balance refresh) and letting his favorite music help him to spiral into the positive (the Joy Kit reframe) turned on energy boosters Josh hadn't even known he had.

To renew Josh's spirit, we had to probe deeply into his psyche. After he worked through the macro renew exercises, he told us that, while he loved helping people as a doctor, he also felt that medicine smothered his creative side. He immersed himself in the excitement of Broadway shows and secretly yearned to write a play himself. The thought of being a doctor and a playwright at the same time, however, seemed laughable to him. He found it difficult to take his own passion to write seriously. We assured him that stranger things have happened and encouraged him to sign up for the writing class described in a brochure he kept on his bedside table.

We also helped Josh look for micro adjustments that can help him integrate the professions of doctor and playwright. Through this thought process, he realized that his job allowed him to meet a wide variety of people every day. This diverse stream of humanity provides the perfect creative resource for his dramatic writing. He now sees each patient (even the cranky ones!) as a whole person—not only as an individual with a particular mind, body, spirit, and medical history, but also as a potential fictional character with a unique personality that can be brought to life onstage. He treasures his patients' hopes and dreams as well as their idiosyncratic gestures and distinct turns of phrase. Now Josh can practice his character development skills at work in addition to honing them during his classes and writing time on weekends and evenings. Best of all, he experiences a secret jolt of delight when a patient sparks his imagination in addition to drawing on his medical expertise.

Josh's Techniques

Let's recap the micro-resilience techniques Josh used:

- Refocus Your Brain—He started with the zone refocus to reduce interruptions by e-mail that distracted from patients and filled him with annoyance

- Reset Your Primitive Alarms—He used the labeling reset to reduce anxiety spikes as new patients arrived

- Reframe Your Attitude—A quick Reversi reframe boosted his positive feelings about new patients and complemented the reset techniques he used; he also periodically played Broadway show tunes as a Joy Kit reframe

- Refresh Your Body—Josh micromanaged his metabolism with healthful food and frequently hydrated with the water he took to work with him; he also set silent alarms on his phone for refresh breaks

- Renew Your Spirit—The macro techniques clarified Josh's purpose as a healer and encouraged him to acknowledge a parallel creative aspiration; the (micro) schedule renew helped him weave his writing impulse into his busy clinic days

Each tiny shift gave Josh more energy for the techniques that followed. Overall, his micro-resilience work gave him the capacity to improve his macro-resilience issues, too. He now eats better, sleeps better, and exercises regularly. He enjoys his weekends and has time to make friends. Taken together, small changes across all five Frameworks transformed the quality of both Josh's work and his personal life.

This made a dramatic difference in my life. It's not just one thing, it's the combination of everything. Now it's my new flow, my new groove. Would you believe I'm able to do my charts as I go? I think that has a lot to do with my new energy level and my increased focus. I still give my patients one-on-one interaction; I talk to them, tell a joke, and we both smile. I'm not overwhelmed. And when I'm done, I'm done. My life has turned upside down in terms of that. This is the best thing to happen to me.

Putting It All Together: Tips

1. Review all five Frameworks and identify your biggest pain points—the things you most want to change.

Do they include mental overload? Emotional hijacks? Hair-trigger reactions? Exhaustion? A lack of purpose? Use the checklist in Appendix I to discover what you need most.

2. Choose one of the Frameworks as a starting point, then choose the techniques in that Framework that you want to try first. Most people don't end up using every idea in each Framework. Personalize the techniques to your needs.

3. Put specific reminders for micro adjustments on your calendar or phone, or on an app. The more you view these techniques as regular habits, the easier they will be to access when you urgently need them in reaction to a crisis.

4. Pick a second Framework and follow the same steps as for the first.

5. For your third Framework, choose one that addresses an area in which you think you're doing pretty well. You may eat healthful foods and drink lots of water, for example, but do you stay refreshed when things get hectic? Or you may feel purposeful in a general way, but is your purpose connected to the things on your schedule? Is purpose fueling your energy level hour by hour during the day?

6. Combine techniques from several different Frameworks. Josh, for example, added positive, upbeat music to his mini snack breaks, thus combining tips from Refresh Your Body and Reframe Your Attitude.

7. Anchor your micro-resilience habits to things you already do to make them "stickier." For example, do the deep breathing exercises from the conscious relaxation reset right before you take a shower in the morning or while you're on your daily conference call in the afternoon. Drink your morning coffee from a mug emblazoned with a word or picture that conveys your sense of purpose.

8. Don't worry that your adjustments are too small. Dr. B. J. Fogg, a behavioral scientist at Stanford University, sings the praises of very small changes because they "limbo" under the bar of our resistance and therefore require less motivation. Most people make their changes bigger than they need to be.

9. Precision helps habits stick, too. A technique used repeatedly in the same way for the same length of time and in the same situation is converted into an automatic activity. It then no longer requires the conscious effort of the prefrontal cortex but rather becomes an autopilot function managed by the basal

ganglia. Lock the techniques into your subconscious with repetition and precision. Yes, changing things around is fun, but in this case it will reduce your chances of sticking with it.

10. Invite others to participate in the process. If your family, friends, and coworkers practice micro-resilience with you, you're more likely to stay on track. You could even create your own micro-resilience group— perhaps with friends, as a book club, or with coworkers, as a lunch meeting. The group can convene periodically and discuss this book one or two chapters at a time. Alternatively, choose a single person to be your "accountability buddy" and meet weekly by phone or in person.

11. Visit our website, www.microresilience.com, to find our latest tools and virtual coaching programs that can help you integrate Micro-Resilience into your life.

BETH'S STORY

At times our program participants embrace the material so completely that they truly make it their own; some take it much further than we ever imagined possible.

This was the case with Beth, the manager of a pension fund for a large nonprofit organization near Philadelphia.

When we first met Beth, she was a typically ambitious financial whiz, eager to get ahead in the rat race.

> I was the kind of person who calculated every move down to the last possible second. How late can I leave the house in order to beat the traffic on Route 22? I knew what time certain entrances and exits typically clogged up, so I would backtrack from there. How late can I sleep? How long do I have in the shower? If the line at Starbucks is too long, I'll get my coffee at the Dunkin' Donuts instead.
>
> I did the same thing at the office. I was always a pile of Jell-O by the end of the day.

Beth came to us looking for a more healthful way to live her life. She hoped micro-resilience would help her become less...tightly wound. She signed up for the introductory program and launched herself into all the Frameworks at once. As she did with everything, Beth devoured the material with zeal.

During one of our coaching calls, however, we could tell right away that something had dramatically shifted for Beth. Gone were her usual frenetic speech and pervasive energy. Instead we heard a calm, introspective, almost serene voice come through the speakerphone. Beth had just experienced one of those moments we all try never to think about but still secretly dread—the split second after which nothing in your life will ever be the same. Beth had been diagnosed with aggressive, invasive breast cancer.

> **I walked into the doctor's office certain every-thing would be fine. I've never been a hypochon-driac, so I really hadn't thought much about the diagnosis. Every now and then, I had thoughts of "what if," but they were easily dismissed. The doctor said the biopsy was just a precaution. It's probably nothing. I envisioned the doctor smil-ing at me, dismissing my lump as a mere cyst—a normal growth, totally harmless. Then, all of a sudden, you're sitting there on a really uncom-fortable green vinyl chair in a cold, sterile room, and all the blood in your face drains down into your shoes. You have cancer. You could die soon. At the very least, your life for the foreseeable future will be a torturous hell.**

After a few weeks of going through Elisabeth Kübler-Ross's five stages of grief (anger, denial, bargain-ing, depression, and acceptance), Beth developed a plan to cope with her predicament. It would have been easy for her to sink into the depths of despair as she went through a seemingly endless sequence of diagnoses, treatments, setbacks, and further treatments, but she decided instead to use micro-resilience to treat her attitude alongside her medical regimen—to stay positive, to stay focused, and to stay . . . *Beth*.

> **Prior to the diagnosis, I thought of micro-resilience as a way of achieving a better work-life balance, a way to maintain all the commitments I have—family, church, career. But now it's about taking care of myself and not collapsing. This all came out of nowhere and has completely redefined how I move through my days. But I am determined that it will not define *me*. I want to move on to, "What does it mean to live with this and truly thrive?" That's where micro-resilience comes in.**

Beth had to cut back her work schedule to accommodate chemotherapy and other treatments, and she wanted to make her shortened workdays much more efficient. So she created a "Life after Cancer Daily Plan." One of her first steps was to reorganize her schedule, allowing herself to more smoothly ease through her day. The time-crunched rush would be a thing of the past. To help her stick to her new routine, Beth set reminder alarms on her phone that would go off throughout the day. The alarms displayed clever titles that made her smile.

Beth's daily plan looked like this:

■ 7:00 a.m.: "Me Time." Brief period of peace while lying in bed. Ease up. Allow body and mind to awaken from sleep.

■ 7:15 a.m.: "Yay for Yoga." Fifteen minutes of stretches, followed by shower and a balanced breakfast.

■ 8:30 a.m.: "Mindful Commuting." Use the travel time in the car to prepare for the day. Focus.

■ 10:00 a.m., 1:00 p.m., 3:05 p.m.: "Happy Hydration." Keep water going all day—more often during high-stress periods and when high-order, critical thinking is essential.

■ 12:30 p.m.: "Refresh." Eat a green and healthful lunch. Never skip meals.

■ 3:00 p.m.: "Refresh Again." Eat a low-glycemic snack to keep energy levels up.

■ 5:30 p.m.: "Home Is Where They Love You." Pack up, leave the office, and don't linger. Be on the road by 5:30. You have worked the hours you needed to—*go home!*

■ 6:00 p.m.: "Zoom with a View." Enjoy the scenery as you leave the highway and weave through the Pennsylvania cornfields.

■ 7:30 p.m.: "Thanks for All That We Have Received." Have a nutritious dinner, and don't eat too late.

■ 9:30 p.m.: "Gear Down." Break the night-owl habit. Prepare for bed. Make time for prayer and contemplation.

■ 10:00 p.m.: "Nighttime Repair." Get in bed. Let go of stress. Think happy thoughts. Prepare to dream.

This exact schedule won't work for everyone, but the basic message is clear: allow yourself to pay attention to your mind and body, hour by hour, in little ways.

Another important adjustment for Beth was that she had to embrace the notion of being "helpable," a challenge she didn't want to tackle on her own. She counted on support from her close friends and family, of course, but she also decided to create a broader circle of friends and acquaintances who could provide reinforcement and encouragement. She established a private Facebook page called "Beth's Breast Cancer Warriors," and soon

she had more than a hundred connections who provided her with all kinds of support. Some of these "warriors" were cancer survivors like her, but most were just
regular folks who wanted to help. The group included
a dog-sitter who walked the family pet when Beth had
to go in for treatments, a person who cooked and ran
errands when Beth was tired and run-down, and a person who could always get Beth to laugh when she called
on the phone.

**I'm someone who always wants to be the helper,
so it's been very hard to let myself be vulnerable
and admit I can't do it all on my own. But to see
the joy on my friends' faces when they're able to
do something for me helps cement my purpose:
to create a community of people who can lean
on each other.**

We've often seen people who accept help from others
reap similar rewards. One woman who went through our
program is married to a man in the US Army Reserve.
When he was called up to fight in Iraq, she was sud-
denly left with two children to care for—in addition to
her full-time job. Some neighbors offered to organize a
group that would cook a few meals a week for her and
her family. At first she was insulted. "Don't they think I

can take care of my kids?" she thought. But her friends kept at it, and she finally relented. The big "aha" came when she saw the joy her neighbors experienced as they helped her. After all, her husband had been called to serve his country. To refuse her neighbors' help would be to deny them the opportunity to do their patriotic duty as well. They wanted to do something, however small, to show their gratitude for his service.

Beth's cancer is now in remission. She's gone through a radical double mastectomy, long bouts of chemotherapy, and other treatments, but she and her warriors live a strong, happy life.

I would never have chosen this journey, but working with you to reframe this diagnosis has helped me deal with issues I've had all my life. It's a weird silver lining, but I'm so thankful for it.

PUTTING IT ALL TOGETHER: CONCLUSION

When we coach groups of people in our program, we typically convene a series of six virtual discussions either weekly or biweekly. In the first meeting we talk about the Frameworks and techniques. As the sessions progress, everyone designs his or her daily plan, uses it for a week, then further refines the process as the course goes on. The participants share ideas with the group, ask for help with challenges, and add nuances that get them into their micro-resilience "groove."

Most of these micro-resilience techniques are so simple a child could understand them and practice them after only a few minutes of instruction. They are quick, easy, and effective. Integrating micro-resilience into your daily life so that it becomes habit, however, takes a bit more effort. Even our own use of the techniques was somewhat hit-and-miss when we first developed the program. We knew the benefits intellectually, and we enjoyed the results, but it was easy to get distracted and forget these minor shifts in a busy day.

Remember the last time you upgraded your computer? It may have irritated you to change the way you do things on the keyboard and adjust to a new configuration on the screen, but once you got the hang of it you focused only on all the great things the upgrade could do. You forgot another way had ever existed. It's the same with micro-resilience: implement your daily plan as if you had installed an upgrade to your human operating system. It may seem inconvenient to set a few reminders on your phone or meet with a friend for coffee to discuss how it's going, but that investment in time will be repaid handsomely when your brainpower increases, your energy soars, and you know you're the best *you* you can be. One of our participants explained the transformation this way:

> **This work is truly transformational. It is more than the sum of its individual parts. Most programs try to make a lofty change in your life, to fix you, or to make you someone different. Micro-resilience helped me find the authentic, real me. And it taught me how to keep that me front and center, making it part of my daily habits, my routine, the fabric of my everyday life.**
>
> **Imagine an animal that is dirty all over, covered in muck. When someone comes along and washes away all the junk, the animal suddenly feels amazing. It can move, live, love, be healthy. It is not necessarily more beautiful, but it is more of who it really is. And how cool is it to be more of who you are? I think that is what all of us would love to be.**

We think so, too.

Afterword

When we dream, we dream that micro-resilience will one day be a program used throughout the world. Imagine fewer global corporations using fear to push their people into burnout, but instead creating a new culture of micro-resilient high performance fueled by positivity, vitality, and purpose. Imagine politicians and voters less hijacked by the awfulizing that narrows their vision, decreases collaboration, and engenders distrust of those who look different from them.

We could be living in an environment where our leaders more often use their prefrontal cortexes to make important decisions than their amygdalae. Instead of Type A organizational cultures, we could have cultures that are "Type A Positive"—still based on putting in long hours and hard work, but also on doing so more efficiently and, therefore, more productively. The research we shared shows that you can stand on higher ground and still achieve, compete, and win...perhaps win more. Micro-resilience, then, becomes the new world's competitive advantage.

We began this process by hunting through numerous branches of research to find simple techniques that would reduce the consistent physical exhaustion, mental debilitation, and spiritual fatigue we observed in the leaders and organizations we serve in our business. These techniques certainly address that goal, but what we also see in the rearview mirror is that our collection of small adjustments harnesses and focuses the most evolved aspects of our humanity. The last hundred years have radically transformed the lifestyle we humans live. The process of evolution, which has historically adapted all species to new realities, is far too slow to refurbish our brain structures or alter old physiological responses to keep up with the demands of modern society—particularly as we move further into the new millennium. However, armed with knowledge, awareness, and a series of baby steps, we can retrain ourselves without waiting for evolutionary change to catch up. We can focus and feed the advanced parts of our neurologic systems, rein in the hijacks of the primitive lizard brain, and use positivity and purpose to support advanced and constructive behaviors.

Think of micro-resilience as an upgrade to our human operating system. The real people who participated in our case studies experienced more than just "feeling better" or "working better," which was what we'd expected to see. They described becoming "more me" and experiencing a whole new quality of living.

Now that we better understand the impact of this program, we have widened our focus. In addition to corporate executives, we are working with nonprofit leaders across the globe. We provide resilience training to people who deal with families affected by incarceration, the empowerment of women and girls globally, wellness in disadvantaged areas, and more. Imagine these champions for a better planet, typically overworked and underpaid, getting the kinds of boosts described by Josh, Emily, or Priya, and sharing these benefits with their hardworking teams. We are developing programs with a major health-care system to investigate whether micro-resilience can improve patient outcomes while making life better for our medical heroes. We are collaborating with an after-school program to discover how these techniques can help the next generation learn and grow. Micro-resilience can supercharge efforts to solve some of our society's most thorny challenges.

We coined the term *Micro-Resilience*, gathered the research to explain how it works, and fine-tuned our methods for coaching people to make the shift. To reach our dream of a world upgraded and more resilient, we need this movement to catch on. To have other people writing about it, spearheading original research, and spreading the word would be the biggest compliment we could receive.

In a world that values being all you can be, with Micro-Resilience we can all be more.

If you want to join us, share Micro-Resilience with your organization, or even become certified to train others, please visit: www.microresilience.com.

Acknowledgments

Writing *Micro-Resilience* has been a team effort. Our process spanned more than seven years, beginning long before we put pen to paper. The development included phases for research, conceptual design of the program, initial rollout, assessments of the impact, further innovation, and the compilation of detailed case studies. We are grateful to the many people who have contributed to the quality of the material you see on these pages.

Dr. Joan Borysenko gave us advice and support early in the process. Her seminal research, along with her passion and tenacity, paved the road that we—and many others—have followed. Joan also introduced us to Dr. Jane Leserman, who guided us in the design and collection of metrics as we tested the impact of micro-resilience on groups of people in large organizations, and gave feedback on the manuscript's science sections.

Instructional design expert Carol Delisi came on board at two different junctures to help us create engaging ways to teach Micro-Resilience and strengthen the overall structure of the courses. We feel the benefits of her contributions in everything we do with this program.

Daniya Kamran-Morley worked side by side with us for more than a year on every aspect of this book. She assisted in the ideation and clarification of each Framework and technique. Daniya coordinated everything related to the program's participants, including enrollment, follow-up interviews, and organization of the mountains of data we generated. In places, some of Daniya's writing is woven into ours. In many ways, her incredible intellect raised the bar and pushed us to a new level of excellence.

When we decided to create a virtual training program that would bring micro-resilience education, coaching, and support to a wider audience, we consulted with an amazing brain trust of technology experts, entrepreneurs, and investors, including Jennifer Mitrenga, Aneesh Varma, Raj Date, Mark A. Floyd, Gregg Brockaway, Kat Utecht, Rameet Chawla, Steve Klein, Irem Mertol, Devrin Carlson-Smith, John and Maria Chrin, Dr. Lisa Cook, Dennis Boyle, Vincent Brown, Dr. Janet Reid, Kristine Mullen, Sarah Jacobson, and Milton

Howard. Thanks to this brilliant group for their valuable time, their wisdom, and their amazing overall contributions, not only to our project, but also to the world. Tremendous thanks also go to our virtual-training project team, who made our ideas a reality: Brooke Schepker, Ming Yang, Will Jones, Emily Minner, Adam Kuhn, Mike Saddoris, Irma Rodela, Dr. William Ryan, Edyta Wiesner, Omar Guzman, Charlie Neiman, our social media guru Joi Branch, and our special leader in sales and marketing, Trudy Menke.

We want to express our deepest thanks to all the anonymous participants in the Micro-Resilience program who graciously allowed us to follow their progress for our case studies. These folks opened their lives, their hearts, and their minds to us more freely than we ever imagined they would. Though not all their stories are featured in the book, we learned a great deal from the unique wisdom of each one.

We sincerely appreciate the special stories told to us by US secretary of health and human services Sylvia Mathews Burwell and US senator Kirsten Gillibrand that illustrate the power of micro-resilience concepts on a global scale.

Strong, detailed feedback is a golden gift for any author. Dr. Wendy Suzuki, a professor at New York University's Center for Neural Science, gave us critical advice on the elements of the manuscript that cover research into the brain. We received extensive comments and feedback from our friends and associates who participated in early rounds of testing, in particular Dr. Debra Clary, Wendy Dowd, A. J. Hubbard, Lisa Lewellen, John Brown, and Corey Blakey. Our dear friends Susanne Scherman and Dr. David Polsky also read the manuscript and gave insightful feedback on form, structure, and content.

Other key members of our team include our wonderful editor at Hachette Book Group, Adrienne Ingrum—our literary Olympic coach who continuously pushes us to better our best. Barbara Clark joined us toward the end of the process for some critical final touches and the close editing we needed to get this project over the finish line. Our agent, Richard Pine, is always there with advice, support, and encouragement. Rolf Zettersten, Patsy Jones, Laini Brown, Katie Conners, and the rest of the Hachette family have been our collaborators for four books now, pushing us to new heights each time around. We know that these long-term relationships are rare and special in the world of book publishing, and we are grateful to Hachette for always providing an environment that makes our best work possible.

We couldn't have done any of this without Emily Halper, our trusted chief of staff, who protected our writing time on the calendar, managed our complex web of relationships, helped us in the final stages of the manu-script, and kept us sane during the process.

Most heartfelt thanks to our three daughters, Darcy, Katharine, and Ella, who listened to our ideas, patiently tolerated all the weekends and evenings we spent holed up writing, and supported us every step of the way with comfort, respect, and, most importantly, love.

And finally, we are thankful to God, our continuous source of strength, courage, perseverance, and resilience.

Appendix 1

Micro-Resilience Checklist: What Do You Want to Tackle First?

Refocus

____ My to-do list never gets shorter

____ I am frequently mentally exhausted

____ Demands on my mental resources keep increasing

____ Interruptions waste too much time

Reset

____ I "awfulize" about things that haven't happened

____ I resist change

____ Confrontations leave me worn out

____ A sudden shift in deadlines gets me worked up

Reframe

____ I am stuck in a negative rut

____ I have some tough people issues at work

____ I hold on to negative feelings after a bad day

____ I would like to be more confident

Refresh

____ I have an intense travel schedule

____ I feel drained and lose energy during the day

____ I skip meals in order to work

____ I resort to eating junk food because it's convenient

Renew

____ I can't seem to balance my life and my work

____ I wonder whether all my efforts are worth it

____ I feel uninspired, as though I'm losing steam

____ I want more from my life and my work

Appendix II

Micro-Resilience Techniques: A Quick Reference Guide

REFOCUS YOUR BRAIN

Zone Refocus

Research results are clear: most multitasking drains energy and reduces efficiency, thereby undermining accuracy, creativity, and the quality of work. Yet the typical office is full of distractions: e-mail, coworkers' conversations, unexpected emergencies, and more. To counteract this, try the following:

- Designate a separate space—a zone—where others know they should not disturb you

- Establish visual signals that will let coworkers know you are concentrating and do not want to be interrupted

- Communicate your boundaries and limits

- Block out "zones" on your calendar that are reserved for intense focus on a single task—no calls, no e-mails, no contact with the outside world

- Use an app or a plug-in to cancel or silence alerts for e-mails, text messages, and calls; most of these will still allow you to be reached in case of an emergency

Off-Load Refocus

Maximize your brain's capacity by off-loading information from it as much as possible. Use paper, whiteboards, and tablets to take notes, draw, and map your thinking process. Don't save this technique for complex issues only—make it a nonstop habit.

- Draw idea bubbles (see page 39) and take notes on paper or on a whiteboard during meetings and conversations

- Position your notes and idea bubbles where everyone can see them

- Keep a small notebook with you everywhere you go

- Keep a record of your idea bubbles and whiteboard notes by taking a picture of them with your phone and saving them in a designated folder

Decision Refocus

When we make numerous decisions all day long, the quality of those decisions falls off rapidly as the hours go by. By changing the timing of our decisions, we can allocate cognitive resources where they are needed most. We can also avoid squandering our precious brainpower on unimportant things by making fewer decisions. This helps reduce anxiety and fosters clear, efficient decision making.

- Make the most important decisions early in the day

- Reduce the number of decisions you make while distracted or tired

- Reduce the overall number of decisions you make by simplifying your routine

- Use checklists for things you do repeatedly, such as as packing and grocery shopping

Exercise Refocus

When your body is active, your brain is more alert, you have more creativity, and your memory works better than when you are sedentary. Studies show that even five minutes of walking can help spur ideas. Dancing for just twenty minutes has been shown to increase brainpower for hours afterward.

- On a day when your brain needs to be at its best (e.g., when you're giving a speech, writing a proposal, or hosting an important meeting), exercise early to stimulate blood flow, endorphins, and creativity

- Don't overdo it: exercising to the point of exhaustion or for more than sixty minutes tends to detract from your brainpower, not improve it

- Develop a repertoire of light exercises you can do at your desk:

  □ *Shoulder rolls*: Roll your shoulders forward three to five times, then roll them backward the same number of times

  □ *Toe lifts*: Raise your toes while keeping your heels firmly on the ground and hold the stretch for thirty seconds or more; you can also do this while standing

  □ *Neck stretches*: Let your head loll over so that your right ear nearly touches your right shoulder, then, using your hand, *gently* press your head a little lower; hold for ten seconds, then relax and repeat on the other side

□ *The heart opener*: Sit on the edge of your chair, then reach behind you and grab the back of the seat with both hands; inhale and puff out your chest, arching your back; if it's comfortable to do so, let your head fall back slightly to stretch your neck; continue to breathe and hold the position for thirty seconds or longer

■ Instead of booking a conference room, conduct a walking meeting through your office campus or around your floor

RESET YOUR PRIMITIVE ALARMS

Labeling Reset

We've always thought that putting feelings into words was helpful in preventing emotional overload. Recent fMRI studies back us up: they show that labeling strong emotions actually reduces the brain's primitive amygdala hijack response and increases activity in the prefrontal cortex, the "advanced" part of the brain, which controls executive function. Just saying to yourself, "I'm angry" or

"I feel threatened" can help you put the brakes on your automatic fight-or-flight programming.

- When a rising tide of emotions threatens to take you off course, stop and put a label (or several) on what you are feeling—during a meeting, before giving a speech, or when provoked by a coworker

- Remember that you have choices about how you feel: if a coworker is rude, you can be angry or compassionate; you can ignore the person or make a joke

- Give a negative feeling a new, positive label: if you feel nervous about a presentation, you can call your anxiety "excitement" or a feeling of "caring intensely"

- Physically step away from a volatile situation if you can; sometimes it is important to be angry, sad, or fearful, but you can still be in the driver's seat

Conscious Relaxation Reset

This reset stops energy drain during the day caused by habitual muscle tension. Conscious relaxation disengages the autonomic responses (fight-or-flight readiness) and allows the mind and body to rest and reenergize.

- Begin with deep-belly breathing:

  - *Sit down*: Make sure you're in a comfortable place, with your feet on the floor

  - *Center yourself*: Put your hand on your abdomen, just above your navel

  - *Exhale*: Let all the air out of your body with a big sigh and relax

  - *Inhale*: As you breathe back in, expand your belly so it pushes your hand outward

  - *Repeat*: Take a few more breaths, focusing all the movement in your belly while you keep your shoulders and chest relaxed

- Deliberately relax your muscles as you do the deep breathing:

  - *Release your shoulders*: With the first breath, release your shoulders as you breathe out

  - *Give in to gravity*: On the next breath, let gravity relax your shoulders even further

    □ *Focus on individual muscles*: Repeat this process from head to toe—neck, arms, legs, feet—and allow the tension to flow down toward the floor and out through your toes

    □ *Finish with a breath*: Inhale and exhale one more time, and pay attention to how relaxed you are

- Add a positive thought, such as one of gratitude or feeling loved, to further reduce the fight-or-flight chain reaction

Sensory Reset

Think of this reset by its nickname—"smells and bells." Because your sense of smell affects your deep limbic system, you can use it to cool down an inflammatory situation. Cinnamon, vanilla, nutmeg, and lavender have been shown to have this effect. The sound of a bell or a familiar song can also interrupt the amygdala hijack.

- Keep a few fragrant items at your desk, such as cinnamon gum or mints, lotion, and herbal tea

- Experiment with scents and sounds that work best for you: Rosemary popcorn? A drop of essential oil rubbed into your palm? A song from your teenage years?

- Kick off meetings on a positive note with a resonant bell, lively music, or flowers

- Be sensitive to perfume or pollen allergies among coworkers

Power Pose Reset

Research shows that by adopting "power poses"—positions that are open and take up space—you can lower your cortisol and raise your testosterone levels significantly, thereby making yourself less afraid and more willing to take on challenges. In predictably stressful situations— such as before you give a speech or presentation, when a coworker behaves disrespectfully, or when you receive bad news from a client—strike a power pose to offset your body's natural stress reaction.

- Sit down with your feet up on a desk and your hands clasped behind your head: do you feel more relaxed and in charge?

- Stand with your legs apart and your hands on your hips: do you feel more powerful?

- Sit down with your hands in your lap, your shoulders hunched over, and your head down: do you feel contracted and closed off?

- View psychologist Amy Cuddy's TED talk, called "Your Body Language Shapes Who You Are," on YouTube or on TED.com

REFRAME YOUR ATTITUDE

Joy Kit Reframe

We keep a medical first-aid kit handy for unpredictable—yet inevitable—cuts and bruises. Similarly, we can put together a Joy Kit that quickly shifts us away from feelings of pessimism, rejection, and frustration into a state of positivity, gratitude, and creativity.

- Make a list of items that inspire joy in you—such as photos, souvenirs, mementos, and music

- Keep these items handy in a bag or a box on your desk; when you experience a down moment, focus on one or two of them to boost your mood

- Create a digital Joy Kit on your computer or phone that contains inspiring articles, songs, pictures, thank-you notes, and other things

■ Enlist a partner who knows where your Joy Kit lives and can point you toward it when you need it—at times, you may not know you need it

■ Make a starter Joy Kit for someone you care about; the recipient can add to and personalize the kit for herself

ABCDE Reframe

A = The event or situation that *activates* you
B = Your *beliefs* about the event or situation
C = The *consequences* of your beliefs
D = The act of *disputing* your beliefs
E = The act of *energizing* your new beliefs

■ Go through the conscious relaxation reset before taking on the ABCDE reframe; you need to deescalate your emotions before you can reframe your attitude

■ Bring another person into the discussion who can help you find a new way to look at the facts

■ Be patient with yourself and the process—it takes time

■ The reframe won't work unless you really want to change your outlook

Reversi Reframe

This technique helps reverse your attitude—from negative to positive—by stimulating new and creative thinking in areas where you may feel limited or blocked.

- On a three-by-five index card, write down the constraint or impediment you are facing

- Flip the card over and write the exact opposite—in the present tense, as if it were true

- Use this new phrase as a springboard for fresh ideas

- Discuss with a friend or your team: you'll be surprised what you can come up with once you challenge your perceived limits

PPP → CCC Reframe

Pessimists see negative situations as *personal, prevalent,* and *permanent*; optimists see negative situations as presenting a *challenge* and a *choice*—and as an opportunity for *commitment*. When we focus on the *challenge* of an obstacle and the *choices* we have, we create a more positive energy than when we feel trapped, helpless, and angry. The question "What are you really *committed* to?" focuses on the desired outcome and the values involved.

- Take the quiz on page 121 to find out where you fall on the optimism-pessimism spectrum

- Practice internalizing the good things that happen instead of the bad things that happen

- In a negative situation, ask yourself:

  □ What is the challenge to be met?

  □ What choices do I have?

  □ What am I committed to?

Daily Reframe

We evolved to respond quickly to threats but slowly to positive events and feelings. Spending time each day with a conscious, intentional, positive focus can significantly increase your baseline level of positivity. When you make a consistent habit of having a positive attitude, studies show, you increase creativity, receptiveness to feedback, and teamwork skills.

- Take ten deep abdominal breaths, then close your eyes and focus on loving yourself and accepting who you are, then send those thoughts to

(a) someone you respect and revere, (b) someone you love, (c) someone you feel neutral about, and (d) someone you dislike

- Write a list of three things you are grateful for every morning

- Write three heartfelt thank-you e-mails every evening

- Make a date with yourself to observe natural phenomena that you would normally take for granted

REFRESH YOUR BODY

Hydration Refresh

We all know we are supposed to drink eight glasses of water a day, but even the most committed of us often put that water bottle aside when we're busy or stressed— exactly the time we most need to hydrate. The brain dehydrates before the rest of the body, so even though you may not feel thirsty, your thinking may seem cloudy or you may have trouble focusing. Take a big drink of water to flood your brain with energy and keep yourself focused, invigorated, and performing at your best.

- Drink water before you get thirsty

- The higher your expenditure of mental, emotional, and physical energy, the more water you should drink

- Keep a water bottle—preferably one with sentimental value—at your desk and carry one on the go

- Put a picture of water on your desk to remind yourself to drink some every time you see it

- Make water more appealing by dropping in some chopped frozen strawberries, a mint leaf or two, or a slice of cucumber

- Drink water when you feel hungry: thirst is sometimes confused with mild hunger

- Drink water in restaurants and alongside caffeinated or alcoholic beverages (they dehydrate)

Glucose-Balance Refresh

Complex executive functions of the brain—which require high levels of energy—developed late in the evolutionary process and are thus the first to go when food is scarce and glucose is low. Balanced and consistent blood sugar levels make it easier to resist our primitive programming. In addition, although the brain uses enormous amounts of glucose, it can't store any for later. Micromanaging our glucose levels for consistency keeps us physically, mentally, and emotionally prepared to go the distance.

- Research the glucose levels of the foods you eat by looking up their glycemic indexes on a reputable chart such as those provided by the Mayo Clinic and the National Institutes of Health

- Choose foods with medium and low glycemic indexes at mealtimes to fuel yourself with sustained energy

- Stay on an even keel by eating a light and healthful snack (100–150 calories) every two to three hours

- Low-glycemic snacks include eggs, hummus, apples, berries, meats, milk, cheese, plums, peaches, nuts, jerky, vegetables, yogurt, nutrition bars, protein shakes, and soy and almond milk

- Carry healthful food with you when you travel

RENEW YOUR SPIRIT

Touchstone Renew

(Only the Micro Renew tools are summarized here. If you wish to revisit the Macro Renew tools, please refer to pages 167–180).

Creating a personal touchstone—a concrete, visual embodiment of your purpose in life and your most important values—gives depth and meaning to your personal and professional activities. It serves to remind you to get back on track when superficial annoyances threaten to distract you from your ultimate goals and values. It also helps you keep the things that inspire you front and center every day.

- Brainstorm—by yourself or with a group—a list of tangible representations of the abstract feelings and ideas that fuel your purpose

- Choose a specific symbol that can instantly move, touch, and inspire you

- Find ways to use your touchstone to keep you focused:

  - Use it as your avatar on social media

  - Use it as the wallpaper or screen saver on your computer or phone

  - Put it on your bathroom mirror, in your car, or in other places where you look every day

- Discuss the touchstone with people at work to bring them back to a sense of purpose

Schedule Renew

Looking at your calendar through the lens of "purpose" can make a tremendous difference in your energy and passion for day-to-day living. If you can raise the percentage of things you do during the week that feel purpose-filled rather than those that make you feel as if you're going through the motions, your energy will correspondingly increase.

- Review your schedule for the week and determine which activities feel the most meaningful

- Eliminate one activity that doesn't feel meaningful, perhaps by delegating it to others

- The following week, eliminate another activity that does not fuel your sense of purpose

- If there are no purpose-filled, meaningful activities on your calendar, add one to each day—even if only for a few minutes at a time

Flow Renew

Rather than eliminating or adding activities on your calendar, consider redesigning some of the things you repeatedly do to boost your energy or even add "flow." Flow can be defined as the state in which you are at one with your work—time seems to fly by, you forget to eat, and you are completely lost in your task.

- Keep a log of your energy levels while performing specific tasks that you do repeatedly during the course of a single week

- At the end of the week, create a graph like the one on page 193 that diagrams your energy levels

- Where your energy is dropping, can you redesign the activity so that it gets you closer to a state of flow?

- View design professor Bill Burnett's webinars on YouTube, called "Design Your Life: Part I" (https://www.youtube.com/watch?v=8bYIQDlWj34) and "Design Your Life: Part II" (https://www.youtube.com/watch?v=qOwAkE0Sdbg)

Bonnie St. John is an Olympian and Rhodes Scholar. She is a keynote speaker and leadership consultant who has guided individuals – from Fortune 500 C-Suites to start-up entrepreneurs – to their performance goals. Her broad media exposure includes *People, Forbes, Essence,* the *New York Times, Today, CNN, CBS News, PBS* and *NPR. NBC News* called her 'one of the five most inspiring women in America'.

Allen Haines served as CEO of several film industry marketing companies. He has advised and coached senior executives at Sony, Disney, IMG, NBC/Universal and Fox.

microresilience.co.uk